STRATEGIES
for Writers
Level B

Authors

Leslie W. Crawford, Ed.D.
Georgia College & State University

Rebecca Bowers Sipe, Ed.D.
Eastern Michigan University

Robert C. Calfee, Ph.D.
University of California, Riverside

Zaner-Bloser

Educational Consultants

Barbara Marinak
Reading Supervisor
Mechanicsburg, PA

Barry Sneed
Master Primary Teacher
Perry, OH

Catherine C. Thome, Ed.D.
English/Language Arts and Assessment Coordinator
Educational Services Division
Lake County Regional Office of Education
Grayslake, IL

Science Content Reviewer

Michael Grote, Ed.D.
Math and Science Education
Columbus Public Schools
Columbus, OH

Teacher Reviewers

Janice Andrus, Chanhassen, MN
Shannon Basner, Hollis, NY
Teressa D. Bell, Nashville, TN
Eve Bilbrey, Nashville, TN
Victoria B. Casady, Ferguson, MO
Kristin Cashman, Mechanicsburg, PA
Jeanie Denaro, Brooklyn, NY
Susan Friedman, Ph.D., Sharon, PA
Katherine Harrington, Mechanicsburg, PA
Dianna L. Hinderer, Ypsilanti, MI

Eleanor Kane, Stow, OH
Jean Kochevar, Minneapolis, MN
Diane L. Nicholson, Pittsburgh, PA
Susan Peery, San Antonio, TX
David Philpot, San Francisco, CA
Jodi Ramos, San Antonio, TX
Jacqueline Sullivan, Sunnyvale, CA
Rita Warden-Short, Brentwood, TN
Emily Williams, Nashville, TN
Roberta M. Wykoff, Stow, OH

Page Design Concepts and Cover Design

Tommaso Design Group

Photo Credits

Models: George C. Anderson Photography

Art Credits

Dave Aikins
pp. 21, 30, 43

Production by Marilyn Rodgers Bahney Paselsky

ISBN 0-7367-1838-9

Zaner-Bloser, Inc., P.O. Box 16764, Columbus, Ohio 43216-6764 (1-800-421-3018)

Printed in the United States of America   04 05 06 07 302 5 4 3 2

NARRATIVE
Writing to Tell a Story About Me

DESCRIPTIVE

Writing to Describe

EXPOSITORY
Writing to Give Information

NARRATIVE

Writing to Tell a Story About Someone Else

PERSUASIVE

Writing to Tell What I Think

Writing to Take a Test

Extra Practice

conventions & Skills

CS I

Writer's Handbook

HB I

NARRATIVE

Writing to Tell a Story About Me

1

Personal Narrative

2

Friendly Letter

Writing a Personal Narrative

Hi, my name is Kyle. I live in Oregon. I'm going to help you write a story about something you did or something that happened to you. I'll explain every step! My teacher says that this kind of writing is called a **personal narrative**.

First, read this personal narrative. It's a good model.

The Day I Learned
to Ride a Bike
by Michele Cho

On Saturday, my dad took me out on my new bike. First, I pedaled. Dad ran behind me and held my bike seat. We did that over and over. Next, Dad let go. I didn't know he wasn't holding on. I just kept riding down the street. All of a sudden, the bike felt different. Then I knew I was riding all by myself. I felt like a race car driver. Dad said he was very proud of me. The last thing I did that day was ride around the block by myself.

Personal Narrative
Rubric

Directions: First, read each question. Then read the answers for each question. Work with a partner to give Michele Cho's narrative 1, 2, or 3 stars on each question.

A rubric can help you decide if a piece of writing needs more work. I'll work with my writing partner, Austin. We'll use this rubric to look at Michele Cho's personal narrative.

Is the topic interesting to the reader?
 **Audience**

Are the events in the story in the right order?
Organization

Does the writer use time-order words to show how one event follows another?
Elaboration

Does every sentence belong in the story?
Clarification

Does every sentence begin with a capital letter and end with a period?
conventions & Skills

★

The topic is not very interesting.

Some of the events in the story are in the right order.

The writer uses a few time-order words to show how one event follows another.

Only some of the sentences belong in the story.

Only a few sentences begin with a capital letter and end with a period.

★★

The topic is interesting.

Most of the events in the story are in the right order.

The writer uses some time-order words to show how one event follows another.

Most of the sentences belong in the story.

Most sentences begin with a capital letter and end with a period.

★★★

The topic is very interesting.

All the events in the story are in the right order.

The writer uses many time-order words to show how one event follows another.

All of the sentences belong in the story.

All sentences begin with a capital letter and end with a period.

Using the Rubric

Directions: Kyle and his writing partner, Austin, used the Personal Narrative Rubric to check Michele Cho's story. Read what they decided about each question on the rubric.

Is the topic interesting to the reader?

We think the writer picked an interesting topic. Lots of our friends have just learned to ride a bike. They know it feels great. The writer explained that feeling when she talked about feeling like a race car driver.

Then I knew I was riding all by myself. I felt like a race car driver.

Are the events in the story in the right order?

All the events in the story are in the right order. The writer starts at the beginning and moves to the last event. Here's what happened first.

First, I pedaled. Dad ran behind me and held my bike seat. We did that over and over.

Does the writer use time-order words to show how one event follows another?

We found many time-order words that show how one event follows another. The words are **first, next, then,** and **last**. Here's an example.

Next, Dad let go. I didn't know he wasn't holding on.

Does every sentence belong in the story?

We think that every sentence belongs in the story. For example, one sentence tells about how proud Michele's father was. This is an important part of the story.

Dad said he was very proud of me.

Does every sentence begin with a capital letter and end with a period?

A capital letter tells that a new sentence is starting. A period tells that a sentence has ended. Every sentence in this story begins with a capital letter and ends with a period. Here is an example.

I just kept riding down the street.

I'm a writer, too! Now I'm going to write my own personal narrative. Read to see how I do it.

Kyle

Name: Kyle
Home: Oregon
Hobbies: swimming, playing checkers
Favorite Subject: social studies
Favorite Book: *Where the Wild Things Are* by Maurice Sendak
Assignment: personal narrative

Gather Ideas

Make a list of interesting topics. Pick one.

Let me show you how I wrote my personal narrative. I started by **prewriting**. That means planning my writing. First, I had to choose my **topic**. The rubric says I need a topic that would be interesting to my readers.

I made a list of topics. Then I wrote some notes about each one. That helped me pick a topic.

Topic

A **topic** is an idea to write about.

My Topics

the day my mom
came home from
the army

my first day of
day camp

~~my first swimming
lesson~~

My Thinking

That was a great day, but a lot
happened. It's too much for one
paper.

That happened last summer! That's
too long ago.

Some of my friends don't know how
to swim. Others have just learned.
This one will be interesting to them!
I'll use this topic.

Stop!
and
Go! Try this yourself on page 6 in the **Practice** the Strategy **Notebook!**

Prewriting

Organize

Make a storyboard to tell what happened.

I had my topic, but I still wasn't ready to write my story. I had to do more prewriting! I knew what happened, but I had to **organize** the events. The rubric said the events in my story need to be in the right order. I decided to draw a **storyboard**. That would help me write the events in my story in order. Look at my story board on the next page.

Storyboard

A **storyboard** uses pictures to show what happens in a story. The pictures show events in the right order.

Topic: My First Swimming Lesson

1

← me

2

3

ORAL LANGUAGE
Talk
With a
Partner
COOPERATIVE LEARNING

Look at Kyle's storyboard. Do you think he showed what happened? Talk with a partner about Kyle's storyboard.

Stop!
and
Go! Try this yourself on page 10 in the **Practice** the Strategy **Notebook!**

Drafting

Write

Use my storyboard. Write sentences to tell what happened first, next, and last.

The storyboard helped me see what happened in my story. Next, I used the storyboard to help me **draft,** or write, my story. I wrote sentences to tell what happened first, next, and last.

My draft tells what happened in the same order as the pictures on my storyboard. My draft is on the next page.

[DRAFT]

My First Swimming Lesson

My first swimming lesson was hard I was afraid of the water. we had to learn to float I wouldn't even try it. I could put my head in the water, but I couldn't lift my feet. my teacher was Ms. Lindsay She was really nice to me. My Aunt Laney is nice, too. She said she would help by holding me up in the water She put her hands around my waist. Then I put my head back in the water. I put my feet up. We did that over and over Then Ms. Lindsay asked me to try it without her. I did it. I floated all by myself. everyone clapped. I went home and rode my bike.

Talk With a Partner · ORAL LANGUAGE · COOPERATIVE LEARNING

Talk with a partner about Kyle's draft. Does the draft match his storyboard? Do you think he told what happened first, next, and last? Tell why or why not.

Stop! and Go! Try this yourself on page 14 in the **Practice the Strategy Notebook!**

Revising
Add
(Elaborate)

Add time-order words to show how one event follows the other.

After I write my first draft, I always **revise** it. That means I try to make my writing even better. First, I check to see if anything is missing. I use sticky notes to add the information.

I read the rubric again and saw that I needed **time-order** words to tell how one event follows another. I added the words **first, next,** and **finally** to help my readers. Here's my revised draft.

Time-Order Words

Time-order words show how events follow each other. Some time-order words are **first**, **next**, **then**, and **finally**.

[DRAFT]

My First Swimming Lesson

My first swimming lesson was hard I was afraid of the water. we had to learn to float I wouldn't even try it. I could put my head in the water, but I couldn't lift my feet. my teacher was Ms. Lindsay She was really nice to me. My Aunt Laney is nice, too. She said she would help by holding me up in the water She put her hands around my waist. Then I put my head back in the water. I put my feet up. We did that over and over Then Ms. Lindsay asked me to try it without her. I did it. I floated all by myself. everyone clapped. I went home and rode my bike.

First,

Next,

Finally,

ORAL LANGUAGE
Talk
With a Partner
COOPERATIVE LEARNING

Can you think of other ways to make Kyle's draft better? Talk about it with a partner.

Stop!
and
Go! Try this yourself on page 18 in the **Practice** the Strategy **Notebook!**

Revising

Take Out
(Clarify)

Take out sentences that don't help tell what happened.

Next, I talked to my writing partner, Austin. Austin and I read each other's writing. Then we talk about how to make the writing better. Sometimes, we add sentences. Other times, we take out sentences.

The rubric said that I needed to make sure all my sentences help tell what happened. Austin saw two sentences that he thought didn't belong! He was right. I crossed them out. Here's how my story looks now.

[DRAFT]

My First Swimming Lesson

My first swimming lesson was hard I was afraid of the water. we had to learn to float I wouldn't even try it. I could put my head in the water, but I couldn't lift my feet. my teacher was Ms. Lindsay She was really nice to me. My Aunt Laney is nice, too. She said she would help by holding me up in the water She put her hands around my waist. Then I put my head back in the water. I put my feet up. We did that over and over Then Ms. Lindsay asked me to try it without her. I did it. I floated all by myself. everyone clapped. I went home and rode my bike.

First,

Next,

Finally,

Stop!
and
Go! Try this yourself on page 19 in the **Practice** the Strategy **Notebook!**

Editing
Proofread

Make sure I start each sentence with a capital letter and end it with a period.

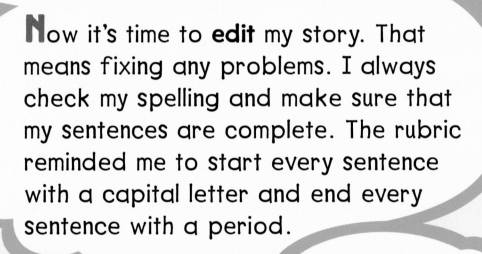

Now it's time to **edit** my story. That means fixing any problems. I always check my spelling and make sure that my sentences are complete. The rubric reminded me to start every sentence with a capital letter and end every sentence with a period.

Look on the next page to see how my story looks now.

conventions & Skills

Writing Sentences Correctly

Every sentence begins with a **capital letter**. Every sentence ends with a **period** (**.**) unless the sentence asks a question or shows strong feelings.

Extra Practice
See **Capitalizing and Punctuating Sentences** (pages CS 2–CS 3) in the back of this book.

[DRAFT]

My First Swimming Lesson

My first swimming lesson was hard. I
was afraid of the water. we had to
learn to float. I wouldn't even try it. I
could put my head in the water, but I
couldn't lift my feet. my teacher was
Ms. Lindsay. She was really nice to
me. My Aunt Laney is nice, too. She   **First,**
said she would help by holding me up
in the water. She put her hands
around my waist. Then I put my head   **Next,**
back in the water. I put my feet up.
We did that over and over. Then Ms.
Lindsay asked me to try it without   **Finally,**
her. I did it. I floated all by myself.
everyone clapped. I went home and
rode my bike.

**Stop!
and
Go!** Try this yourself on page 20 in the **Practice ∧ Notebook!**
the Strategy

Narrative Writing • Personal Narrative   **29**

Publishing

Share

Add my story to the class album.

After I edited my story, I made a neat final copy to share with others. This is called **publishing**. Here's what else I did to publish my story.

1. I copied my paper in my best handwriting. I made sure to make all the changes and put my name on it.

2. I read my story aloud in class.

3. I drew a picture to go with my story.

4. My teacher added my picture and story to our class album.

My First
Swimming Lesson
by Kyle

My first swimming lesson was hard. I was afraid of the water. We had to learn to float. I wouldn't even try it. I could put my head in the water, but I couldn't lift my feet. My teacher was Ms. Lindsay. She was really nice to me. She said she would help by holding me up in the water. First, she put her hands around my waist. Then I put my head back in the water. Next, I put my feet up. We did that over and over. Then Ms. Lindsay asked me to try it without her. Finally, I did it. I floated all by myself. Everyone clapped.

USING the Rubric for Assessment

Go to page 22 in the **Practice** the Strategy **Notebook!** Use the rubric to check Kyle's personal narrative.

Writing a
Friendly Letter

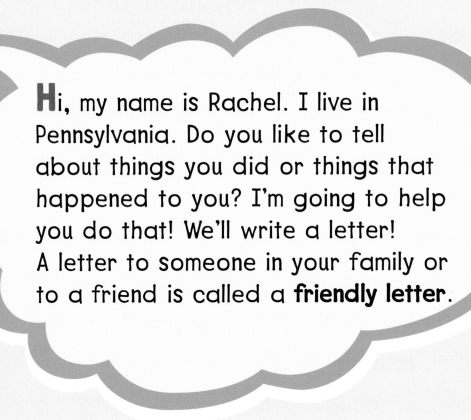

Hi, my name is Rachel. I live in Pennsylvania. Do you like to tell about things you did or things that happened to you? I'm going to help you do that! We'll write a letter! A letter to someone in your family or to a friend is called a **friendly letter**.

First, read this friendly letter. It's a good model.

MODEL
FRIENDLY LETTER

Heading

12 Oak Road
Hamlin, PA 18427
May 4, 20—

Greeting

Dear Grandma,

Body

Today Mr. Li took our class to the Pine Brook Dairy. First, we saw the barn, the cows, and the place where the cows are milked. Then a farmer told us about the cows and the foods we get from them, like milk, cheese, and ice cream. Next, everyone got a cup of ice cream made from the milk. Last, we saw some baby cows with their mothers. I had a fun day. I wanted to tell you all about it.

Closing Love,

Signature Charlie

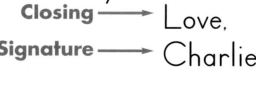
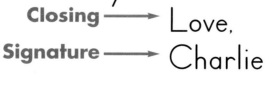

Friendly Letter
Rubric

Directions: First, read each question. Then read the answers for each question. Work with a partner to give Charlie's friendly letter 1, 2, or 3 stars on each question.

A rubric can help you decide if a piece of writing needs more work. We'll use this rubric to look at Charlie's friendly letter.

Is the topic interesting to the reader?

Audience

Does the letter tell what happened first, next, and last?

Organization

Does the letter have interesting details?

Elaboration

Does every sentence help tell what happened?

Clarification

Does the letter have all five parts? Are they all used correctly?

Conventions & Skills

★

The topic is not very interesting to the reader.

The letter tells some of what happened, but the order is unclear.

There are a few interesting details.

Some of the sentences help tell what happened.

The letter has a few of the five parts. They are not all used correctly.

★★

The topic is mostly interesting to the reader.

The letter tells what happened, but not always in the right order.

There are some interesting details.

Most of the sentences help tell what happened.

The letter has most of the five parts. Most of them are used correctly.

★★★

The topic is very interesting to the reader.

The letter tells what happened first, next, and last in the right order.

There are many interesting details.

All of the sentences help tell what happened.

The letter has all five parts. They are all used correctly.

Using the Rubric

Directions: Rachel and her writing partner, Lauren, used the rubric to check Charlie's friendly letter. Read what they decided.

Is the topic interesting to the reader?

We thought Charlie's grandmother would be very interested in his topic. A visit to a dairy is pretty cool. Charlie's first sentence tells his grandmother what his letter is about.

Today Mr. Li took our class to the Pine Brook Dairy.

Does the letter tell what happened first, next, and last?

The letter tells everything that happened! Charlie uses the words **first, then, next,** and **last** to tell the events in the right order. Here is an example.

First, we saw the barn, the cows, and the place where the cows are milked.

Does the letter have interesting details?

We found a lot of interesting details. Charlie even tells which foods we get from cows.

Then a farmer told us about the cows and the foods we get from them, like milk, cheese, and ice cream.

Does every sentence help tell what happened?

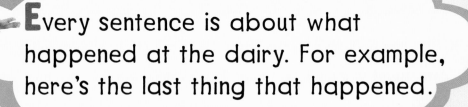

Every sentence is about what happened at the dairy. For example, here's the last thing that happened.

Last, we saw some baby cows with their mothers.

Does the letter have all five parts? Are they all used correctly?

Yes, the letter has all five parts of a friendly letter: a heading, a greeting, a body, a closing, and a signature. Charlie uses all five parts of the friendly letter correctly. Here are his closing and signature.

Love,
Charlie

I'm a writer, too! Now I'm going to write my own friendly letter. Read to see how I do it.

Name: Rachel
Home: Pennsylvania
Hobbies: writing stories, dancing
Favorite Subject: math
Favorite Book: *Madeline* by Ludwig Bemelmans
Assignment: friendly letter

Gather Ideas

Think about who will read my friendly letter and what I want to say.

I started by **prewriting,** or planning my letter. The rubric reminded me that my topic should be interesting to my reader. I decided to write to my friend Jade. Then I thought about what I wanted to say.

Friendly Letter

A **friendly letter** has five parts.
- The **heading** tells the address of the writer and the date the letter was written.
- The **greeting** tells who will read the letter. It starts with *Dear* and ends with a comma.
- The **body** tells what the writer wants to tell the reader.
- The **closing** ends the letter. It begins with a capital letter and ends with a comma.
- The **signature** tells who wrote the letter.

I made a list of some things I could tell Jade in a letter. Then I wrote some notes about each one. See how I decided what to write about.

My Ideas

my trip to Ohio

what I did yesterday

my babysitter's wedding

My Thinking

A lot happened on that trip. We were gone two weeks. There's too much to tell.

I just stayed home yesterday. Not much happened. Yesterday wouldn't make a very interesting topic.

That was fun! Jade probably never went to a wedding like that. I'll write about that!

Stop!
and
Go! Try this yourself on page 24 in the **Practice** the Strategy **Notebook!**

Prewriting
Organize

Make a storyboard to tell what happened.

I had decided to write to Jade about my babysitter's wedding. Then, I looked at the rubric again. It reminded me that I needed to **organize** my letter to tell what happened.

I decided to draw pictures of what happened at the wedding to make a **storyboard**. Look at my storyboard on the next page.

Topic: My Babysitter's Wedding

Look at Rachel's storyboard again. Do you think it shows the events that happened? Talk about Rachel's storyboard with a partner.

Drafting
Write

Use my storyboard. Write sentences to tell what happened first, next, and last.

The rubric says to make sure I tell what happened first, next, and last. I followed the order of the pictures on my storyboard to **draft,** or write, my letter.

I wrote about the pictures on my storyboard, and I added some other things, too. Read my draft on the next page.

Dear Jade,
    Last week, I went to my babysitter's wedding. She will move to New Jersey. First, the bride and groom stood under a huppah. A huppah is a pretty tent. Then the groom broke a glass. A big party came next. Everyone danced in a circle. Last came a big meal and more dancing. It was so much fun! I had fun at a picnic last week, too.
                    Your friend,
                    Rachel

Talk with a partner about Rachel's draft. Do you think the draft tells what happened first, next, and last? Tell why or why not.

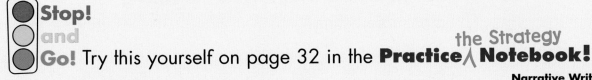

**Stop!
and
Go!** Try this yourself on page 32 in the **Practice** the Strategy **Notebook!**

Revising
Add
(Elaborate)

Add details to make my letter more interesting.

When I **revise,** I change my writing to make it better. I ask myself if there is anything I need to add. I use sticky notes to add information.

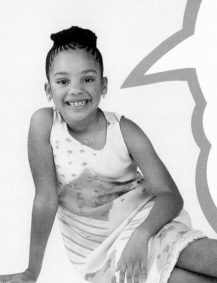

The rubric said that my letter needed interesting **details**. I can tell more about what the huppah looks like. I can tell how the groom breaks the glass. I can tell more about the dancing. I decided to add these details to my letter.

Details

Details are words that tell more. Details describe things. They make the writing more interesting.

Dear Jade,

   Last week, I went to my babysitter's wedding. She will move to New Jersey. First, the bride and groom stood under a huppah. A huppah is a pretty tent. Then the groom broke a glass. A big party came next. Everyone danced in a circle. Last came a big meal and more dancing. It was so much fun. I had fun at a picnic last week, too.

              Your friend,
              Rachel

with open sides

with his foot

People lifted up the bride and groom on chairs.

Can you think of other ways to make Rachel's draft better? Talk about it with a partner.

ORAL LANGUAGE
Talk
With a
Partner
COOPERATIVE LEARNING

Stop!
and
Go! Try this yourself on page 36 in the **Practice** the Strategy **Notebook!**

Narrative Writing • Friendly Letter

Revising

Take Out
(Clarify)

Take out sentences that don't help tell what happened.

Next, I talked to my writing partner, Lauren, again. Lauren reminded me that the rubric said all my sentences should help tell what happened.

Lauren read my letter. She found two sentences that don't belong. They don't tell what happened at the wedding. I crossed them out. Look at my draft on the next page to see my changes.

[DRAFT]

Dear Jade,

Last week, I went to my babysitter's wedding. ~~She will move to New Jersey.~~ First, the bride and groom stood under a huppah. A huppah is a pretty tent. Then the groom broke a glass. A big party came next. Everyone danced in a circle. Last came a big meal and more dancing. It was so much fun. ~~I had fun at a picnic last week, too.~~

Your friend,
Rachel

with open sides

with his foot

People lifted up the bride and groom on chairs.

Editing

Proofread

Make sure I wrote all five parts of my friendly letter correctly.

When I **proofread,** I always check my spelling and my sentences. This time I also checked to be sure that I have all five parts of a friendly letter. Oops, I forgot to write the heading! I added it where it belongs in my letter.

Parts of a Friendly Letter

Heading ⟶ 6 Fair Street
Los Osos, CA 12345
August 6, 20—

Dear Keiko, ⟵ **Greeting**

This is the main part. ⟵ **Body**

Closing ⟶ Your pal,
Signature ⟶ Robert

Extra Practice
See **Parts of a Friendly Letter**
(pages CS 4–CS 5) in the back of this book.

Here's how my letter looked after I edited it.

Proofreading Marks

≡ Make a capital letter.　　— Take out something.
/ Make a small letter.　　⊙ Add a period.
∧ Add something.　　¶ New paragraph

[DRAFT]

19 North Street
Liberty, PA 43210
June 27, 20--

Dear Jade,

Last week, I went to my babysitter's wedding. ~~She will move to New Jersey.~~ First, the bride and groom stood under a huppah. A huppah is a pretty tent. Then the groom broke a glass. A big party came next. Everyone danced in a circle. Last came a big meal and more dancing. It was so much fun. ~~I had fun at a picnic last week, too.~~

Your friend,
Rachel

with open sides

with his foot

People lifted up the bride and groom on chairs.

Stop! and Go! Try this yourself on page 38 in the **Practice** the Strategy ∧ **Notebook!**

Publishing

Share

Address an envelope. Ask an adult to help me mail my letter.

I published my letter by making a neat final copy of it. I made all my changes, and I used my best handwriting. Here's what else I did to publish my friendly letter.

1. I shared my letter by reading it aloud in class. A lot of kids in my class never saw a wedding like my babysitter's before.

2. I addressed an envelope to Jade.

3. I folded the letter and put it in the envelope.

4. I put a stamp on the envelope. My dad helped me mail my letter to Jade.

19 North Street
Liberty, PA 43210
June 27, 20--

Dear Jade,

    Last week, I went to my babysitter's wedding. First, the bride and groom stood under a huppah. A huppah is a pretty tent with open sides. Then the groom broke a glass with his foot. A big party came next. Everyone danced in a circle. People lifted up the bride and groom on chairs. Last came a big meal and more dancing. It was so much fun!

Your friend,
Rachel

USING the Rubric for Assessment

Go to page 40 in the Practice the Strategy Notebook! Use the rubric to check Rachel's friendly letter.

Social Studies
Your Own Writing
NARRATIVE

Use what you learned in this unit to write your own personal narrative, friendly letter, or both! Try these ideas.

- Use **Your Own Writing** pages in the *Practice the Strategy Notebook*.
- Pick a topic below, and write something new.
- Choose another idea of your own.

Follow the steps in the writing process. Use the Personal Narrative Rubric on pages 22–23 in the *Practice the Strategy Notebook* or the Friendly Letter Rubric on pages 40–41 in the *Practice the Strategy Notebook* to check your writing.

Personal Narrative	**Friendly Letter**
• how you celebrated your birthday	• to a friend about how you celebrated a special family custom or tradition
• what you did or saw at a holiday parade	• to a relative about your trip to a special museum or library

portfolio

School–Home Connection

Keep a writing folder. Add **Your Own Writing** pages to your writing folder. You may want to take your writing folder home to share.

DESCRIPTIVE

Writing to Describe

1 Descriptive Paper

2 Compare-and-Contrast Paper

Writing a
Descriptive Paper

Hi, my name is Jessica. I live in Ohio. I'm going to help you describe something. When we describe, we use our five senses. We tell about what we see, hear, touch, taste, and smell. We can describe a person, a place, or a thing. This kind of writing is called a **descriptive paper**.

First, read this descriptive paper. It's a good model.

MODEL · DESCRIPTIVE PAPER

Wrinkles
by Andy Washington

Wrinkles is a puppy. He is a special kind of dog called a Shar-Pei. Wrinkles is funny to look at because he has so much skin! It makes flaps and folds all over his body. He has a big face but tiny ears. His tail sticks up. It curls like a ribbon. He has a light brown coat with short, straight hair. When I pet him, his fur feels like a toothbrush. Wrinkles smells sweet right after his shampoo, but his bark sounds sharp!

Descriptive Paper

Rubric

Directions: First, read each question. Then read the answers for each question. Work with a partner to give Andy Washington's descriptive paper 1, 2, or 3 stars on each question.

A rubric can help you decide if a piece of writing needs more work. We'll use this rubric to look at the model.

Is the subject of the paper interesting?

Audience

Does the paper use the five senses?

Organization

Does the writer use enough describing words?

Elaboration

Do all the sentences tell about the subject of the paper?

Clarification

Does every sentence begin with a capital letter and end with the correct punctuation?

conventions & Skills

★

The subject of the paper is not very interesting.

The paper uses one of the five senses.

There are a few describing words.

Some of the sentences tell about the subject.

Some of the sentences begin and end correctly.

★★

The subject of the paper is interesting.

The paper uses a couple of the five senses.

There are some describing words.

Most of the sentences tell about the subject.

Most of the sentences begin and end correctly.

★★★

The subject of the paper is very interesting.

The paper uses the five senses.

There are many describing words.

All of the sentences tell about the subject.

All of the sentences begin and end correctly.

Using the Rubric

Directions: Jessica and her writing partner, Kayla, used the rubric to check Andy Washington's descriptive paper. Read what they decided.

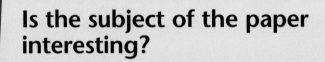

Is the subject of the paper interesting?

We thought the writer picked a great subject! Almost everyone would be interested in reading about such a cool puppy. Here is an example of what makes Wrinkles an interesting subject.

Wrinkles is funny to look at because he has so much skin! It makes flaps and folds all over his body.

Does the paper use the five senses?

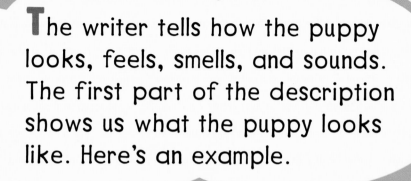

The writer tells how the puppy looks, feels, smells, and sounds. The first part of the description shows us what the puppy looks like. Here's an example.

He has a big face but tiny ears.

Does the writer use enough describing words?

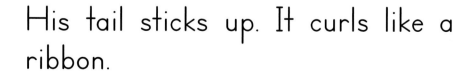

The writer uses many describing words. For example, we can picture Wrinkles' tail because of these describing words.

His tail sticks up. It curls like a ribbon.

Do all the sentences tell about the subject of the paper?

All the sentences tell about the subject, Wrinkles. Here's an example.

When I pet him, his fur feels like a toothbrush.

Does every sentence begin with a capital letter and end with the correct punctuation?

The writer begins every sentence with a capital letter and ends every sentence with correct punctuation. This sentence ends with an exclamation point because the sentence shows strong feelings.

Wrinkles is funny to look at because he has so much skin!

Prewriting

Gather Ideas

Choose a subject to describe. Make a list to tell what I know about it.

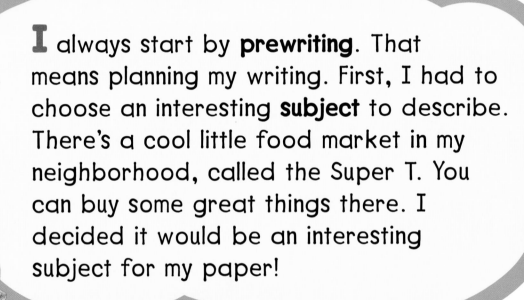

I always start by **prewriting**. That means planning my writing. First, I had to choose an interesting **subject** to describe. There's a cool little food market in my neighborhood, called the Super T. You can buy some great things there. I decided it would be an interesting subject for my paper!

Next, I made a list of things I know about the Super T. Then I wrote what I know about each thing on my list.

Subject of a Paper

The **subject** of a paper is the thing you are writing about.

My List

neat fruits, like mangoes and kiwis

strings of chili peppers

herbs

people talking in lots of different languages

music playing

cash register beeping

spices

What I Know

how they look, feel, and smell

how they look and smell

how they look and smell

how they sound

how it sounds

how it sounds

how they look and smell

Stop! **and** **Go!** Try this yourself on page 42 in the **Practice** the Strategy **Notebook!**

Prewriting

Organize

Use my list to make a five senses chart.

Next, I talked to my writing partner, Kayla, about how to **organize** my list. That means to put the things on my list in order.

We decided that a **five senses chart** is a good way to do that! I put all the things I can see into one part of my chart. I put all the things I can hear into another part. I did the same with "taste," "feel," and "smell." My five senses chart is on the next page.

Five Senses Chart

A **five senses chart** helps you organize things based on how they look, sound, taste, feel, and smell.

Subject of My Paper: The Super T

I can **see**	• mangoes and kiwis • strings of chili peppers	• herbs • spices
I can **hear**	• people talking • music playing	• cash register beeping
I can **taste**	I can't taste anything at the Super T unless I buy it.	
I can **touch** (feel)	• mangoes and kiwis	• chili peppers
I can **smell**	• mangoes and kiwis • chili peppers	• herbs • spices

Read Jessica's five senses chart again. Do you think it will help her use the five senses to write her paper? Talk about it with your partner.

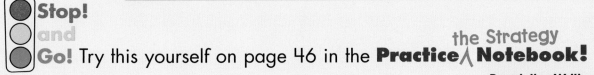

Stop!
and
Go! Try this yourself on page 46 in the **Practice** the Strategy **Notebook!**

Descriptive Writing • Descriptive Paper   **67**

Drafting
Write

Use my five senses chart. Write sentences to describe the subject of my paper.

Now I was ready to **draft,** or write, my descriptive paper. I used my five senses chart on page 67 to write sentences to describe my subject, the Super T. It gave me ideas for how to use the five senses to describe things.

I didn't worry about making mistakes. I knew that I could fix them later. Read my draft on the next page.

[DRAFT]

The Super T

The Super T is a food market on my street it is filled with great food! My favorite food is ice cream. Fruits and vegetables are in the front. You can see cool fruits like mangoes and kiwis. You can see strings of chili peppers. you can smell the mangoes and the peppers. You can feel the kiwis. My father eats a whole melon by himself. You can also smell fresh herbs and spices for cooking what do you hear in the Super T you can hear people talking in different languages. There's music playing and the cash register beeping!

ORAL LANGUAGE
Talk With a Partner
COOPERATIVE LEARNING

Talk with a partner about Jessica's draft. Do you think it made the Super T real for her reader? Tell why or why not.

Stop!
and
Go! Try this yourself on page 50 in the **Practice** the Strategy **Notebook!**

Revising

Add
(Elaborate)

Add describing words to make my paper more interesting.

After I write my draft, I always read it again. Then I **revise** it. That means I change my draft to make my writing even better. Sometimes I add better words or more information.

The rubric reminded me that I needed to use **describing words** to make my paper interesting. I want my reader to see, feel, smell, and hear the things I'm writing about. Here's how I revised my draft.

Describing Words

Describing words help the reader understand how something looks, sounds, feels, tastes, or smells.

[DRAFT]

The Super T

The Super T is a food market on my street it is filled with great food! My favorite food is ice cream. Fruits and vegetables are in the front. You can see cool fruits like mangoes and kiwis. You can see strings of chili peppers. you can smell the mangoes and the peppers. You can feel the kiwis. My father eats a whole melon by himself. You can also smell fresh herbs and spices for cooking what do you hear in the Super T you can hear people talking in different languages. There's music playing and the cash register beeping!

red, green, and purple

spicy

fuzzy

sweet

Stop! **and** **Go!** Try this yourself on page 54 in the **Practice** the Strategy **Notebook!**

Revising
Take Out
(Clarify)

Take out sentences that don't tell about the subject of my paper.

I talked to my writing partner, Kayla, again. Kayla and I always read each other's writing. Then we talk about how to make our writing better. I wanted to make sure I didn't have sentences that didn't tell about my subject.

Kayla saw two sentences that don't tell about the subject of my paper. The sentence about my favorite food and the sentence about my father don't describe the Super T. I crossed out those sentences. Here's how my paper looks now.

[DRAFT]

The Super T

The Super T is a food market on my street it is filled with great food! ~~My favorite food is ice cream.~~ Fruits and vegetables are in the front. You can see cool fruits like mangoes and kiwis. You can see strings of chili peppers. you can smell the mangoes and the peppers. You can feel the kiwis. ~~My father eats a whole melon by himself.~~ You can also smell fresh herbs and spices for cooking what do you hear in the Super T you can hear people talking in different languages. There's music playing and the cash register beeping!

red, green, and purple

spicy

fuzzy

sweet

ORAL LANGUAGE
Talk
With a Partner
COOPERATIVE LEARNING

Can you think of other ways to make Jessica's draft better? Talk about it with a partner.

Stop!
and
Go! Try this yourself on page 55 in the **Practice** the Strategy **Notebook!**

Editing

Proofread

Make sure I start each sentence with a capital letter and end it with correct punctuation.

Now it's time to **edit** my paper. That means fixing mistakes. I **proofread** my paper by reading it and checking for mistakes. I always check my spelling and make sure that my sentences are complete. This time I wanted to be sure that I started and ended every sentence correctly. Read my edited paper on the next page.

conventions
&Skills

Writing Sentences Correctly

- Every sentence begins with a **capital letter**.
- A sentence that **tells something** ends with a **period**. (.)
- A sentence that **asks a question** ends with a **question mark**. (?)
- A sentence that **shows strong feelings** ends with an **exclamation point**. (!)

Extra Practice
See **Writing Sentences Correctly** (pages CS 6–CS 7) in the back of this book.

Proofreading Marks

≡ Make a capital letter.

/ Make a small letter.

∧ Add something.

— Take out something.

⊙ Add a period.

¶ New paragraph

[DRAFT]

The Super T

The Super T is a food market on my street⊙ it is filled with great food! ~~My favorite food is ice cream.~~ Fruits and vegetables are in the front. You can see cool fruits like mangoes and kiwis. You can see strings of ∧chili peppers. ≡you can smell the∧mangoes and the∧peppers. You can feel the∧kiwis. ~~My father eats a whole melon by himself.~~ You can also smell fresh herbs and spices for cooking⊙ ≡what do you hear in the Super T?∧≡you can hear people talking in different languages. There's music playing and the cash register beeping!

red, green, and purple

spicy

fuzzy

sweet

Publishing
Share

Post my descriptive paper on our class bulletin board. Add a drawing of my subject.

After I edited my paper, it was time to **publish** it. That means to share it with others. I made a neat final copy. I shared my descriptive paper by reading it in class. Here's what else I did to publish my descriptive paper.

1. I copied my paper in my best handwriting. I made sure to make all my changes and put my name on it.

2. I drew a picture of the Super T.

3. I labeled parts of my picture.

4. My teacher put my paper and picture on the class bulletin board.

The Super T
by Jessica

The Super T is a food market on my street. It is filled with great food! Fruits and vegetables are in the front. You can see cool fruits like mangoes and kiwis. You can see strings of red, green, and purple chili peppers. You can smell the sweet mangoes and the spicy peppers. You can feel the fuzzy kiwis. You can also smell fresh herbs and spices for cooking. What do you hear in the Super T? You can hear people talking in different languages. There's music playing and the cash register beeping!

USING the Rubric for Assessment

Go to page 58 in the **Practice** the Strategy **Notebook!** Use the rubric to check Jessica's descriptive paper.

Writing a
Compare-and-Contrast Paper

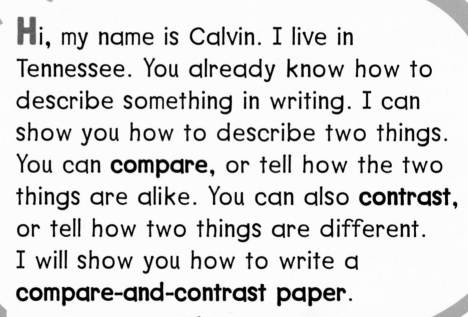

Hi, my name is Calvin. I live in Tennessee. You already know how to describe something in writing. I can show you how to describe two things. You can **compare,** or tell how the two things are alike. You can also **contrast,** or tell how two things are different. I will show you how to write a **compare-and-contrast paper.**

AaBbCc

First, read this compare-and-contrast paper. It's a good model.

MODEL
COMPARE-AND-CONTRAST PAPER

A Movie Theater and a Classroom
by Nora Hernandez

A movie theater and a classroom are alike and different in many ways. Here is how they are alike. People sit down in both places. They watch the front of the room. They look at a big screen or a big chalkboard. They usually don't leave until a bell rings or the movie is over. Here is how the two places are different. A movie theater is dark and quiet. Everyone watches the movie. A classroom is lit up. It is noisy! People of all ages may go to the same movie theater. A classroom usually has people of about the same age. A classroom has a teacher. A movie theater doesn't have a teacher. It has actors on a screen.

Compare-and-Contrast Paper

Rubric

Directions: First, read each question. Then read the answers for each question. Work with a partner to give Nora Hernandez's compare-and-contrast paper 1, 2, or 3 stars.

A rubric can help you decide if a piece of writing needs more work. We'll use this rubric to look at Nora Hernandez's compare-and-contrast paper.

Does the writer choose two interesting things to compare and contrast?

Audience

Does the paper tell how the things are alike first, and then tell how they are different?

Organization

Does the writer use enough describing words?

Elaboration

Does every sentence either compare or contrast the two things?

Clarification

Are all the contractions written correctly?

★

The two things are not very interesting.

The paper mixes up all the comparisons and contrasts.

The writer uses very few describing words.

Some of the sentences compare or contrast the two things.

Some of the contractions are written correctly.

★★

The two things are interesting.

The paper mixes up some of the comparisons and contrasts.

The writer uses some describing words.

Most of the sentences either compare or contrast the two things.

Most of the contractions are written correctly.

★★★

The two things are very interesting.

The paper tells how the things are alike first, and then tells how they are different.

The writer uses many describing words.

All of the sentences either compare or contrast the two things.

All of the contractions are written correctly.

Using the Rubric

Does the writer choose two interesting things to compare and contrast?

The writer picked two interesting things to compare and contrast. We know what a movie theater and a classroom are like. We didn't expect them to have so much in common! Here's the beginning of the paper.

A movie theater and a classroom are alike and different in many ways. Here is how they are alike. People sit down in both places. They watch the front of the room.

Does the paper tell how the things are alike first, and then tell how they are different?

Yes, the paper first tells about ways that a movie theater and a classroom are alike. After that, it tells about how they are different. Here's where the second part starts.

Here is how the two places are different.

Does the writer use enough describing words?

We think that there are enough describing words. The words **dark** and **quiet** describe the movie theater. The words **lit up** and **noisy** tell about the classroom.

A movie theater is dark and quiet. Everyone watches the movie. A classroom is lit up. It is noisy!

Does every sentence either compare or contrast the two things?

Every sentence in this paper helps the reader understand how the two places are alike or different. Look at this example.

A classroom has a teacher. A movie theater doesn't have a teacher. It has actors on a screen.

Are all the contractions written correctly?

All the contractions are correct. The sentence below has the word **don't,** which is a contraction for the words **do** and **not**.

They usually don't leave until a bell rings or the movie is over.

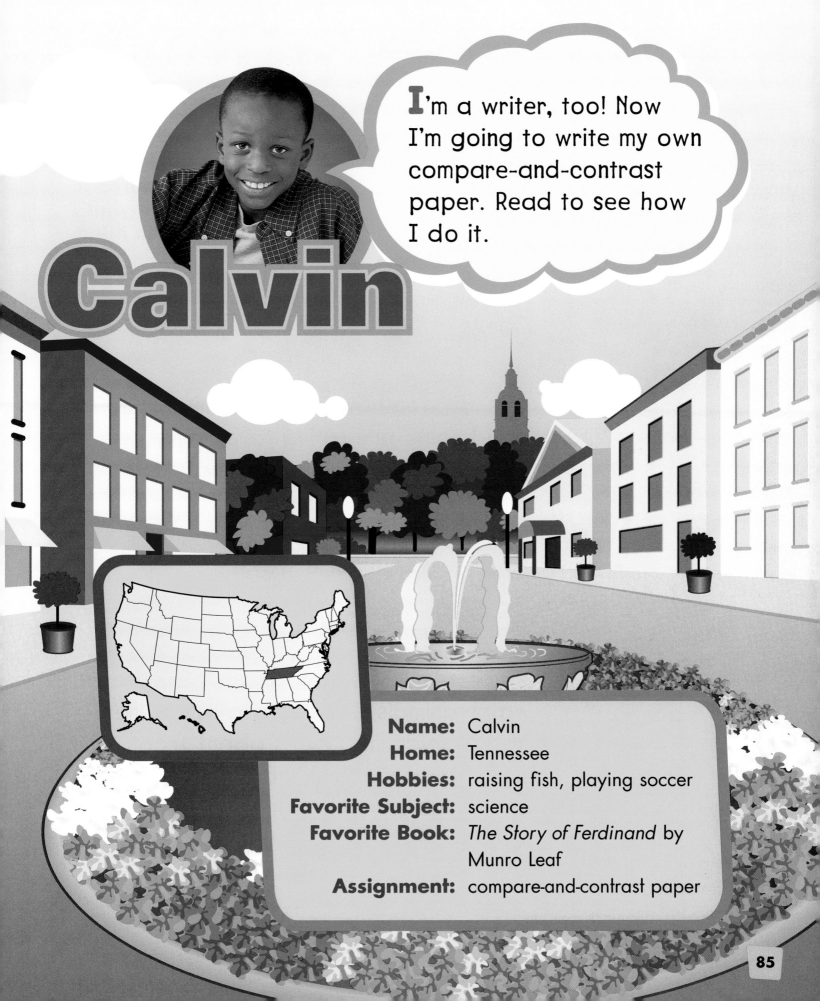

I'm a writer, too! Now I'm going to write my own compare-and-contrast paper. Read to see how I do it.

Calvin

Name: Calvin
Home: Tennessee
Hobbies: raising fish, playing soccer
Favorite Subject: science
Favorite Book: *The Story of Ferdinand* by Munro Leaf
Assignment: compare-and-contrast paper

Gather Ideas

Choose two things to compare and contrast. Make lists to tell what I know about each thing.

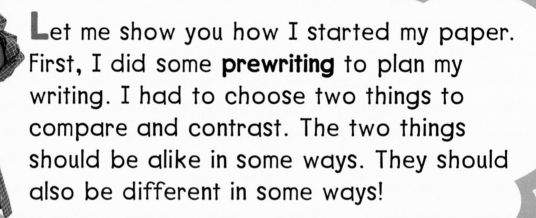

Let me show you how I started my paper. First, I did some **prewriting** to plan my writing. I had to choose two things to compare and contrast. The two things should be alike in some ways. They should also be different in some ways!

I chose goldfish and frogs because I like water animals. I made two lists. One is about goldfish. One is about frogs. The lists helped me think about how goldfish and frogs are alike and different. Look at my lists on the next page.

My Lists

Goldfish	Frogs
animals	animals
orange	brownish green
swim	swim
can't walk on land	can hop and leap
can be pets	can be pets
breathe in water	can breathe air
are quiet	croak

Stop!
and
Go! Try this yourself on page 60 in the **Practice** the Strategy **Notebook!**

Prewriting
Organize

Use my lists to make a Venn diagram.

My next prewriting step was to **organize**! The rubric says my paper should tell how two things are alike first, and then tell how they are different. I made a **Venn diagram** to organize my lists for goldfish and frogs.

I drew two big circles. I made the circles cross each other. The inside part that crosses tells how frogs and goldfish are alike. The outside parts tell how they are different. My Venn diagram is on the next page.

Venn Diagram

A **Venn diagram** is made of two circles. The circles show how two things are alike and different.

Goldfish

- orange
- breathe in water
- can't walk on land
- are quiet

Both

- animals
- swim
- can be pets

Frogs

- brownish green
- can breathe air
- can hop and leap
- croak

Talk about Calvin's Venn diagram with a partner. Do you think it shows how frogs and goldfish are alike and different?

Stop!
and
Go! Try this yourself on page 64 in the **Practice** the Strategy **Notebook!**

Drafting

Write

Use my Venn diagram. Write about how the two things are alike. Write about how they are different.

I used my Venn diagram to **draft,** or write, my compare-and-contrast paper. I used the ideas in the middle of my Venn diagram to tell how goldfish and frogs are alike. I used the sides of my Venn diagram to tell how goldfish and frogs are different.

I didn't worry too much about mistakes. I knew I could fix those later. Read my draft on the next page.

Goldfish and Frogs

Goldfish and frogs are alike in some ways. Both are animals. Both can swim. Both goldfish and frogs can be pets. You cant teach them tricks, though! You dont take them for walks either. You can teach a dog tricks. Goldfish and frogs are also different. Most goldfish are orange. Most frogs are brownish green. Some lizards are green. Goldfish cant breathe out of water, but frogs can breathe air. Goldfish cant walk on land, but frogs can hop and leap. Goldfish are quiet, but frogs can croak loudly.

Talk about Calvin's draft with a partner. Do you think it does a good job of comparing and contrasting goldfish and frogs? Tell why or why not.

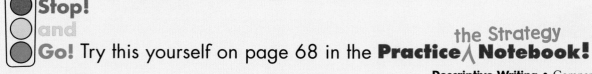

Stop!
and
Go! Try this yourself on page 68 in the **Practice the Strategy Notebook!**

Revising

Add
(Elaborate)

Add describing words to make my paper more interesting.

Next, I **revised** my paper to make it even better. I read my draft carefully to see if I needed to add anything. I read the rubric again, too.

I decided to add some describing words to my draft. That way, my readers would have a better picture of what I mean. I described goldfish and frogs a little more. I added the describing words on sticky notes. Look at the next page and see what I did.

[DRAFT]

Goldfish and Frogs

Goldfish and frogs are alike in some ways. Both are animals. Both can swim. Both goldfish and frogs can be pets. You cant teach them tricks, though! You dont take them for walks either. You can teach a dog tricks. Goldfish and frogs are also different. Most goldfish are orange. Most frogs are brownish green. Some lizards are green. Goldfish cant breathe out of water, but frogs can breathe air. Goldfish cant walk on land, but frogs can hop and leap. Goldfish are quiet, but frogs can croak loudly.

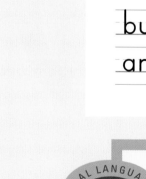

shiny and golden

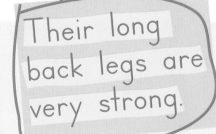

Their long back legs are very strong.

Talk With a Partner

ORAL LANGUAGE COOPERATIVE LEARNING

Can you think of other ways to make Calvin's draft better? Talk about it with a partner.

Stop! and Go! Try this yourself on page 72 in the **Practice** the Strategy **Notebook!**

Revising

Take Out
(Clarify)

Take out sentences that don't help tell how the two things are alike or different.

Next, I talked to my writing partner, Oscar, again. I wanted to be sure that all my sentences help tell about how goldfish and frogs are alike and different. I read my paper to Oscar. He said that two sentences don't tell how goldfish and frogs are alike and different.

He was right! The sentence about dogs doesn't tell about goldfish or frogs! The sentence about lizards doesn't tell about goldfish or frogs either! I crossed out both sentences. Look at my changes on the next page.

[DRAFT]

Goldfish and Frogs

Goldfish and frogs are alike in some ways. Both are animals. Both can swim. Both goldfish and frogs can be pets. You cant teach them tricks, though! You dont take them for walks either. ~~You can teach a dog tricks.~~ Goldfish and frogs are also different. Most goldfish are orange. Most frogs are brownish green. ~~Some lizards are green.~~ Goldfish cant breathe out of water, but frogs can breathe air. Goldfish cant walk on land, but frogs can hop and leap. Goldfish are quiet, but frogs can croak loudly.

shiny and golden

Their long back legs are very strong.

Stop! and Go! Try this yourself on page 73 in the **Practice** the Strategy **Notebook!**

Editing

Proofread

Make sure I have written all contractions correctly.

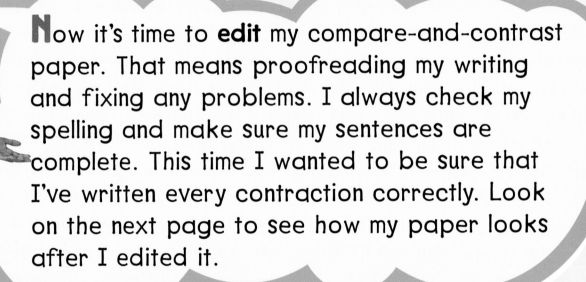

Now it's time to **edit** my compare-and-contrast paper. That means proofreading my writing and fixing any problems. I always check my spelling and make sure my sentences are complete. This time I wanted to be sure that I've written every contraction correctly. Look on the next page to see how my paper looks after I edited it.

Contractions

A **contraction** is made of two words put together. A contraction has an apostrophe ('). The apostrophe shows that one or more letters were left out when the two words were joined.

Two Words	Contraction
do not	don't
I will	I'll
he is	he's
you are	you're

Extra Practice
See **Contractions** (pages CS 8–CS 9) in the back of this book.

Proofreading Marks

≡ Make a capital letter.   — Take out something.
/ Make a small letter.   ⊙ Add a period.
∧ Add something.   ¶ New paragraph

[DRAFT]

Goldfish and Frogs

Goldfish and frogs are alike in some ways. Both are animals. Both can swim. Both goldfish and frogs can be pets. You can't teach them tricks, though! You don't take them for walks either. ~~You can teach a dog tricks.~~ Goldfish and frogs are also different. Most goldfish are orange. Most frogs are brownish green. ~~Some lizards are green.~~ Goldfish can't breathe out of water, but frogs can breathe air. Goldfish can't walk on land, but frogs can hop and leap. Goldfish are quiet, but frogs can croak loudly.

shiny and golden

Their long back legs are very strong.

Stop!
and
Go! Try this yourself on page 74 in the **Practice** ∧ the Strategy **Notebook!**

Descriptive Writing • Compare-and-Contrast Paper   **97**

Publishing

Share

Make a class book with labeled pictures.

The last step is to **publish** my writing. I made a neat final copy that everyone can read. Then I drew a picture of a goldfish and a frog. My teacher put together everyone's papers and drawings. We made a class book of compare-and-contrast papers. We'll all get a turn to take the book home! Here's what else I did to publish my compare-and-contrast paper.

1. I copied my paper with all the changes in my best handwriting. I put my name on it.
2. I drew a picture of a goldfish and a frog.
3. I labeled both pictures.
4. I gave my paper to my teacher. He put it in a book with everyone else's work.

Goldfish

Frog

Goldfish and Frogs
by Calvin

Goldfish and frogs are alike in some ways. Both are animals. Both can swim. Both goldfish and frogs can be pets. You can't teach them tricks, though! You don't take them for walks either. Goldfish and frogs are also different. Most goldfish are shiny and golden orange. Most frogs are brownish green. Goldfish can't breathe out of water, but frogs can breathe air. Goldfish can't walk on land, but frogs can hop and leap. Their long back legs are very strong. Goldfish are quiet, but frogs can croak loudly.

USING the Rubric for Assessment

Go to page 76 in the **Practice** the Strategy **Notebook!** Use the rubric to check Calvin's compare-and-contrast paper.

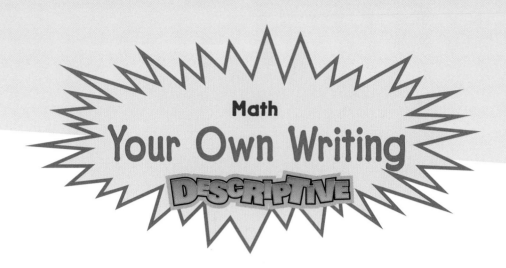

Math
Your Own Writing
DESCRIPTIVE

Use what you learned in this unit to write your own descriptive paper, compare-and-contrast paper, or both! Try these ideas.

- Use **Your Own Writing** pages in the *Practice the Strategy Notebook*.
- Pick a topic below, and write something new.
- Choose another idea of your own.

Follow the steps in the writing process. Use the Descriptive Paper Rubric on pages 58–59 in the *Practice the Strategy Notebook* or the Compare-and-Contrast Paper Rubric on pages 76–77 in the *Practice the Strategy Notebook* to check your writing.

Descriptive Paper
• an alarm clock
• a lunch-size bag of your favorite snack (count the items, too)
• an orange
• a yo-yo

Compare-and-Contrast Paper
• a penny and a quarter
• a square and a triangle
• a ruler and a tape measure
• a bar graph and a pie chart

portfolio

School–Home Connection

Keep a writing folder. Add **Your Own Writing** pages to your writing folder. You may want to take your writing folder home to share.

Writing to Give Information

1 Report

2 How-to Paper

Writing a Report

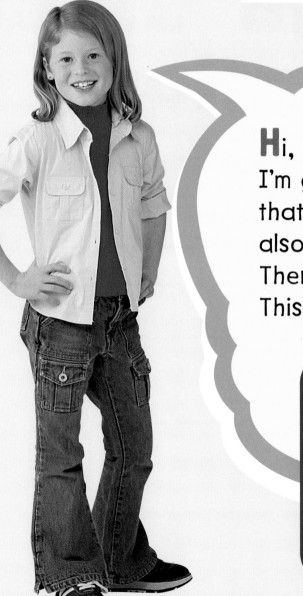

Hi, my name is Emily. I live in Texas. I'm going to help you write a paper that tells **facts** about a topic. You'll also learn to take notes from a book. Then you'll write about your topic. This kind of writing is called a **report**.

Fact

A **fact** is something that can be proved.

Fact: My dog has four legs.

I can prove it by showing you that my dog has four legs.

First, read this report. It's a good model.

Rocks
by Josh Riley

Rocks are everywhere! Did you know that the earth is a great big rock? Mountains are huge rocks, and beaches are tiny broken rocks. Rocks are always changing, but they don't change in the same way that plants and animals do. Some rocks break down and get smaller. Weather and wind wear them away. At the same time, new rocks are always forming. Rocks are made in different ways. Some come from volcanoes. Some come from mud, clay, and sand. Some rocks come from other rocks because of heat and pressure.

Report

Rubric

Directions: First, read each question. Then read the answers for each question. Work with a partner to give Josh Riley's report 1, 2, or 3 stars on each question.

A rubric can help you decide how well a piece of writing does certain things. We'll use this rubric to look at Josh Riley's report.

Does the beginning of the report interest the reader in the topic?

Audience

Does the report name the topic and answer at least two questions about the topic?

Organization

Does the report have enough facts about the topic?

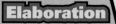
Elaboration

Does every sentence tell about the topic?

Clarification

Are plural nouns written correctly?

conventions & Skills

★

The beginning doesn't really interest the reader in the topic.

The report names the topic, but it doesn't answer any questions about the topic.

The report has very few facts about the topic.

Some of the sentences tell about the topic.

Some plural nouns are written incorrectly.

★★

The beginning interests the reader a little in the topic.

The report names the topic and answers one question about the topic.

The report has some facts about the topic.

Most of the sentences tell about the topic.

Most plural nouns are written correctly.

★★★

The beginning interests the reader in the topic.

The report names the topic and answers at least two questions about the topic.

The report has many facts about the topic.

All of the sentences tell about the topic.

All plural nouns are written correctly.

Using the
Rubric

Directions: Emily and her writing partner, Maya, used the rubric to check Josh Riley's report. Read what they decided.

Does the beginning of the report interest the reader in the topic?

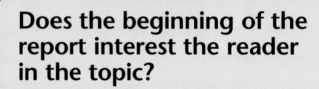

Maya and I thought Josh Riley's report had a great beginning! Here are the first two sentences. They surprised us and made us want to keep reading. We didn't know the earth is a rock. That's really cool!

Rocks are everywhere! Did you know that the earth is a great big rock?

Does the report name the topic and answer at least two questions about the topic?

The topic, rocks, is named in the first sentence. Then the report answers two questions about rocks—what they are and how they are made. These sentences tell about how rocks are made.

Rocks are made in different ways. Some come from volcanoes. Some come from mud, clay, and sand.

Does the report have enough facts about the topic?

This report is filled with facts about the topic. Here are two of them.

Mountains are huge rocks, and beaches are tiny broken rocks.

Does every sentence tell about the topic?

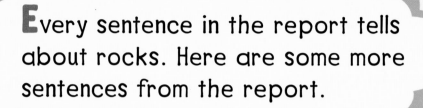

Every sentence in the report tells about rocks. Here are some more sentences from the report.

Some rocks break down and get smaller. Weather and wind wear them away.

Are plural nouns written correctly?

All the plural nouns in the report are written correctly. Can you find the plural nouns in this sentence?

Rocks are always changing, but they don't change in the same way that plants and animals do.

I'm a writer, too! Now I'm going to write my own report. Read to see how I do it.

Emily

Name: Emily
Home: Texas
Hobbies: basketball, word games
Favorite Subject: science
Favorite Books: books about nature
Assignment: report

Prewriting

Gather Ideas

Write two questions I want to answer about my topic. Take notes.

Let me show you how I wrote my report. I always begin by **prewriting**. That means I plan my writing. First, I decided on a topic. I'm interested in the weather, so I decided to write about clouds!

I started by writing two questions I had about clouds. I wanted to find answers to my questions. I got books about clouds from the media center. I took notes to answer my questions. Read my questions and my notes on the next page.

My First Question

What are clouds?

My Second Question

How do clouds change the weather?

My Notes

- Clouds have billions of bits of water.
- Clouds give us rain and snow.
- Water drops fall as rain.
- Some clouds are made of ice crystals.
- Some are made of water drops.
- Ice crystals fall as snow.
- Rain and sun make rainbows!
- Clouds float because the water in them is lighter than the air.

Stop!
and
Go! Try this yourself on page 78 in the **Practice** the Strategy **Notebook!**

Prewriting
Organize

Make a web for each of my questions.

The next step in prewriting was to **organize** my information. I talked to my writing partner, Maya, about a good way to put my notes in order.

Web

A **web** shows information about a topic. Lines connect a middle circle to other circles. The question goes in the middle circle. The answers go in the other circles.

Maya and I decided that two **webs** would be a good way to organize my notes. Here's how I did it. I wrote my topic, **clouds**, at the top. Then I wrote my questions about clouds. Finally, I wrote the facts that answer each question. Look at my webs on the next page.

Expository Writing • Report

My Topic: Clouds

Question 1
What are clouds?

Fact
ice crystals or water drops

Fact
billions of bits of water

Fact
float in the sky because water in them is lighter than air

Question 2
How do clouds change the weather?

Fact
make rain from water drops

Fact
give snow from ice crystals

Fact
give rainbows

ORAL LANGUAGE
Talk
With a Partner
COOPERATIVE LEARNING

Look at Emily's webs again. Do you think this is a good way to organize her facts about clouds? Why or why not? Talk about it with a partner.

Stop!
and
Go! Try this yourself on page 82 in the **Practice** the Strategy **Notebook!**

Drafting
Write

Use my webs. Write sentences to tell about my topic.

Now I was ready to **draft,** or write, my report. My webs helped me organize my ideas and write my draft. I used my webs to write sentences to tell about my topic. First, I wrote sentences that answered my first question. Then, I wrote sentences that answered my second question.

I didn't worry too much about making mistakes this time. I can fix them later. Read my draft on the next page.

Clouds

Clouds are made of billion of tiny water drop's. Clouds can also be made of ice crystal. The water drop's or the ice crystal make a mist. We see that mist as clouds. You can hear thunder before a storm. The drop's and crystal float because they are lighter than air. Clouds give us rain and snow. Snow is great if you like to go sledding! Both rain and snow start out as ice crystal. Some ice crystal fall as snow. Other ice crystal become water drops. They fall as rain. Clouds also give us rainbowes.

Talk about Emily's draft with a partner. Do you think her sentences answer her questions about the topic? Tell why or why not.

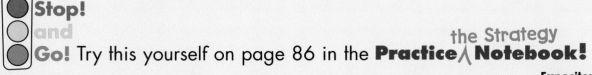

Revising
Add
(Elaborate)

Add facts about my topic.

Revising means changing writing to make it even better. After I write my draft, I always read it again. I make it better by making some changes.

One way to revise a report is to add facts. I'm already telling about rain and rainbows. I could tell how clouds make it rain. I could also tell more about how a rainbow is made. I want to tell my readers many interesting facts! Look at my changes on the next page.

Clouds

Clouds are made of billion of tiny water drop's. Clouds can also be made of ice crystal. The water drop's or the ice crystal make a mist. We see that mist as clouds. You can hear thunder before a storm. The drop's and crystal float because they are lighter than air. Clouds give us rain and snow. Snow is great if you like to go sledding! Both rain and snow start out as ice crystal. Some ice crystal fall as snow. Other ice crystal become water drops. They fall as rain. Clouds also give us rainbowes.

Water drops in clouds can get big and heavy.

Sometimes the sun shines while it's raining. Then we see a rainbow.

Can you think of other ways to make Emily's draft better? Talk about it with a partner.

 Stop! and Go! Try this yourself on page 90 in the **Practice** the Strategy **Notebook!**

Expository Writing • Report

117

Revising

Take Out
(Clarify)

Take out sentences that don't tell about my topic.

Next, I talked to my writing partner, Maya, again. Maya and I always read our writing to each other. Then we talk about how to make our writing better. Maya found two sentences in my report that don't tell about clouds! She was right! I crossed out those two sentences.

Look on the next page to see how my report looks now.

Clouds

Clouds are made of billion of tiny water drop's. Clouds can also be made of ice crystal. The water drop's or the ice crystal make a mist. We see that mist as clouds. ~~You can hear thunder before a storm.~~ The drop's and crystal float because they are lighter than air. Clouds give us rain and snow. ~~Snow is great if you like to go sledding!~~ Both rain and snow start out as ice crystal. Some ice crystal fall as snow. Other ice crystal become water drops. They fall as rain. Clouds also give us rainbowes.

Water drops in clouds can get big and heavy.

Sometimes the sun shines while it's raining. Then we see a rainbow.

Editing

Proofread

Make sure I have written plural nouns correctly.

Next, I **edited** my report. I always proofread to check for mistakes. I check my spelling and my sentences. This time I wanted to be sure that I wrote plural nouns correctly.

Plural Nouns

A **plural noun** is a word that names more than one person, place, or thing. We often add -s to make a plural noun, especially when the noun ends in a consonant. If a noun ends in *x*, *ch*, *s*, or *sh*, add -es. Don't use an apostrophe (') to make a plural noun.

	One		**Plural (More Than One)**
Person:	girl	+ s	girls
	boy	+ s	boys
Place:	park	+ s	parks
	zoo	+ s	zoos
Thing:	rock	+ s	rocks
	wish	+ es	wishes

Extra Practice
See **Plural Nouns**
(pages CS 10–CS 11) in the back
of this book.

Here's how my report looks after I edited it.

[DRAFT]

Clouds

Clouds are made of billions of tiny water drops. Clouds can also be made of ice crystals. The water drops or the ice crystals make a mist. We see that mist as clouds. ~~You can hear thunder before a storm.~~ The drops and crystals float because they are lighter than air. Clouds give us rain and snow. ~~Snow is great if you like to go sledding!~~ Both rain and snow start out as ice crystals. Some ice crystals fall as snow. Other ice crystals become water drops. They fall as rain. Clouds also give us ~~rainbowes.~~
rainbows

Water drops in clouds can get big and heavy.

Sometimes the sun shines while it's raining. Then we see a rainbow.

Stop!
and
Go! Try this yourself on page 92 in the **Practice** the Strategy ∧ **Notebook!**

Publishing
Share

Write my report as an article to add to our class encyclopedia.

After I proofread my paper, I made a neat final copy to **publish** my report. I shared my writing by turning it into an encyclopedia article. My teacher will add my article to our class encyclopedia. Here's what I did to publish my report.

1. I copied my report neatly in my best handwriting. I made sure I included all my changes, and I added my name.

2. After I read my article to the class, I gave it to my teacher. She will put it in our class encyclopedia in ABC order.

Clouds

by Emily

Clouds are made of billions of tiny water drops. Clouds can also be made of ice crystals. The water drops or the ice crystals make a mist. We see that mist as clouds. The drops and crystals float because they are lighter than air. Clouds give us rain and snow. Both rain and snow start out as ice crystals. Some ice crystals fall as snow. Other ice crystals become water drops. Water drops in clouds can get big and heavy. They fall as rain. Clouds also give us rainbows. Sometimes the sun shines while it's raining. Then we see a rainbow.

USING the Rubric for Assessment

Go to page 94 in the Practice the Strategy Notebook! Use the rubric to check Emily's report.

Writing a
How-to Paper

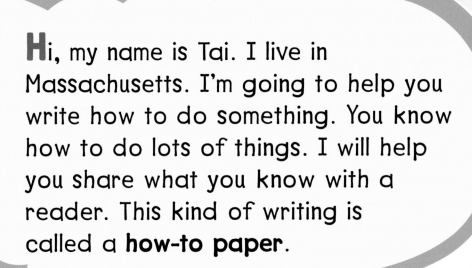

Hi, my name is Tai. I live in Massachusetts. I'm going to help you write how to do something. You know how to do lots of things. I will help you share what you know with a reader. This kind of writing is called a **how-to paper**.

Expository Writing • How-to Paper

First, read this how-to paper. It's a good model.

MODEL
HOW-TO PAPER

How to Make a Piñata
by Leo Graber

Any party can be great if you have a piñata. I'll tell you how you can make one. Get a balloon and a newspaper. You will also need flour, water, paint, and scissors. First, blow up the balloon and tie it. Then, cut the newspaper into small strips. Now, mix the flour and water to make glue. Dip the paper strips in the glue and cover the balloon with them. Put two layers of newspaper on the balloon. Let the piñata dry. You can paint the piñata after it's dry. Cut a flap in the bottom. Take out the balloon. Finally, fill your piñata with candy and tape the flap closed. Now you're ready for a party!

How-to Paper

Rubric

Directions: First, read each question. Then read the answers for each question. Work with a partner to give Leo Graber's paper 1, 2, or 3 stars on each question.

A rubric can help you decide if a piece of writing needs more work. We'll use this rubric to look at Leo Graber's how-to paper.

Is the topic interesting to the reader?

Audience

Are the steps all there and are they easy to follow?

Organization

Does the paper tell enough information?

Elaboration

Are the sentences clear and easy to understand?

Clarification

Are periods, question marks, and exclamation points used correctly?

conventions & Skills

★

The topic is okay, but it could be more interesting to the reader.

Some steps are missing.

The paper leaves out some information.

Some sentences are clear and easy to understand.

Some periods, question marks, and exclamation points are used correctly.

★★

The topic is interesting to the reader.

The steps are all there, but they're hard to follow.

The paper tells most information, but the reader needs to know more.

Most sentences are clear and easy to understand.

Most periods, question marks, and exclamation points are used correctly.

★★★

The topic is really great! It makes the reader want to keep reading.

The steps are all there, and they are easy to follow.

The paper tells everything the reader needs to know.

All sentences are clear and easy to understand.

All periods, question marks, and exclamation points are used correctly.

Using the Rubric

Directions: Tai and his writing partner, Joe, used the rubric to check Leo Graber's how-to paper. Read what they decided.

> **Is the topic interesting to the reader?**

Leo picked an interesting topic. We didn't know you could make a piñata. It made us want to keep reading. Here's how Leo started his how-to paper.

Any party can be great if you have a piñata. I'll tell you how you can make one.

Are the steps all there and are they easy to follow?

We think Leo wrote all the steps for making a piñata. The steps were easy to follow, too. Here's the end of his paper. The word **finally** tells me it's the last step.

Finally, fill your piñata with candy and tape the flap closed.

Does the paper tell enough information?

The paper tells enough. We read everything we needed to know about making a piñata. It even tells how to decorate it.

You can paint the piñata after it's dry.

Are the sentences clear and easy to understand?

The paper is clear and easy to understand. Every sentence is about making a piñata. Here's an example.

First, blow up the balloon and tie it. Then, cut the newspaper into small strips.

Are periods, question marks, and exclamation points used correctly?

All of the sentences are right. They all start with a capital letter and end with correct punctuation. The last sentence ends with an exclamation point.

Now you're ready for a party!

I'm a writer, too! Now, I'm going to write my own how-to paper. Read to see how I do it.

Tai

Name: Tai
Home: Massachusetts
Hobbies: puzzles, playing hockey
Favorite Subject: science
Assignment: how-to paper

Prewriting

Gather Ideas

Think about what I know how to do. Pick something to write about.

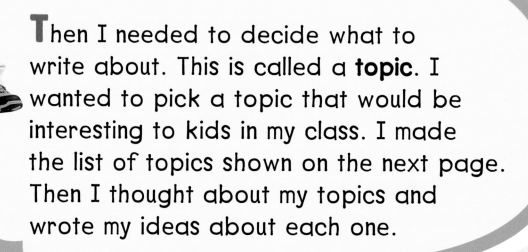

I started by **prewriting,** or planning, my how-to paper. First, I thought about things I know how to do.

Then I needed to decide what to write about. This is called a **topic**. I wanted to pick a topic that would be interesting to kids in my class. I made the list of topics shown on the next page. Then I thought about my topics and wrote my ideas about each one.

My Topics

My Ideas

how to build a snowman

That's nothing new to anyone. We can all do that. It wouldn't make an interesting paper.

how to build a model airplane

That's interesting, but it's too hard. It would take too long to explain.

how to make a jigsaw puzzle

This one is perfect. I think my classmates would be interested in it. I know a great way to make a jigsaw puzzle. I could write about it in a short paper. I'll use this one.

Stop! and Go! Try this yourself on page 96 in the **Practice** the Strategy **Notebook!**

Prewriting

Organize

Decide on the steps. Use an order chain to put the steps in the right order.

The next step in prewriting is to **organize**. I talked with my writing partner, Joe, about the steps to make a jigsaw puzzle.

Then I used an **order chain** to organize my steps. My order chain is on the next page.

Order Chain

An **order chain** helps put the steps of a how-to paper in order from first to last.

Topic: How to Make a Jigsaw Puzzle

First Step Find a picture in a magazine and cut it out.

Next Step Cut a piece of heavy paper the same size as the picture.

Next Step Paste the picture on the heavy paper.

Next Step Wait for the paste to dry. Draw two wavy lines across and two wavy lines down the back of the paper.

Last Step Cut the picture apart on the lines.

ORAL LANGUAGE
Talk With a Partner
COOPERATIVE LEARNING

Read Tai's order chain again. Do you think he covered all the steps? Talk about the order chain with a partner.

Stop!
and
Go! Try this yourself on page 100 in the **Practice** the Strategy **Notebook!**

Drafting
Write
Use my order chain. Write sentences that tell the steps in correct order.

After I had my order chain I was ready to **draft**, or write, my paper.

I followed my order chain as I wrote my draft. I wanted to make sure I told the steps in the right order. I didn't worry about making mistakes. I know I can fix them later. Read my draft on the next page.

[DRAFT]

How to Make a Jigsaw Puzzle
have you ever made a jigsaw puzzle? I have I'll tell you how to do it. First, find a colorful picture in a magazine. Pictures of the outdoors work best. I love the outdoors. Then cut a piece of heavy paper so it's the same size as the picture. Next, paste the picture on the heavy paper. Draw two wavy lines across and two wavy lines down the back of the paper. Finally, cut the picture apart on the lines. now you have the pieces of a puzzle. Mix up the pieces. What a mess Can you put them together again to make the picture

Talk about Tai's draft with a partner. Do you think that it follows his order chain well? Tell why or why not.

Stop!
and
Go! Try this yourself on page 104 in the **Practice** the Strategy **Notebook!**

Revising

Add
(Elaborate)

Add missing information so the reader can follow the steps.

Now it's time to **revise**. When I revise, the first thing I do is add any missing information. Then I use sticky notes to add words or sentences. That makes it easy to see the changes.

When I read my draft, I saw that I forgot to tell the reader to let the paste dry. I added that to my paper to make it easier to follow. Read my changes on the next page.

[DRAFT]

How to Make a Jigsaw Puzzle
have you ever made a jigsaw puzzle?
I have I'll tell you how to do it. First,
find a colorful picture in a magazine.
Pictures of the outdoors work best. I
love the outdoors. Then cut a piece of
heavy paper so it's the same size as
the picture. Next, paste the picture on
the heavy paper. Draw two wavy lines
across and two wavy lines down the
back of the paper. Finally, cut the
picture apart on the lines. now you
have the pieces of a puzzle. Mix up
the pieces. What a mess Can you put
them together again to make the picture

Let the paste dry.

Stop!
and
Go! Try this yourself on page 108 in the **Practice** the Strategy **Notebook!**

Revising
Take Out
(Clarify)

Take out anything that doesn't fit.

Next, I talked to my writing partner, Joe. Joe and I read each other's writing and talk about how to make it better.

When Joe read my draft, he said that the sentence "I love the outdoors" didn't fit. He was right. That sentence isn't about making a jigsaw puzzle. I crossed it out. Here's how my paper looks now.

[DRAFT]

How to Make a Jigsaw Puzzle

have you ever made a jigsaw puzzle? I have I'll tell you how to do it. First, find a colorful picture in a magazine. Pictures of the outdoors work best. ~~I love the outdoors~~. Then cut a piece of heavy paper so it's the same size as the picture. Next, paste the picture on the heavy paper. Draw two wavy lines across and two wavy lines down the back of the paper. Finally, cut the picture apart on the lines. now you have the pieces of a puzzle. Mix up the pieces. What a mess Can you put them together again to make the picture

Let the paste dry.

Can you think of other ways to make Tai's draft better? Talk about it with a partner.

Stop!
and
Go! Try this yourself on page 109 in the **Practice** the Strategy **Notebook!**

Editing

Proofread

Make sure I have used periods, question marks and exclamation points correctly.

Now it's time to **edit,** or fix problems. I always **proofread** my writing to look for problems with spelling and sentences. This time I also made sure I had used periods, question marks, and exclamation points correctly.

conventions & Skills

Periods, Question Marks, and Exclamation Points

Sentences begin with a **capital letter** and end with a **punctuation mark**.

- Telling sentences end with a period. **(.)**

- Asking sentences end with a question mark. **(?)**

- Sentences that show strong emotion end with an exclamation point. **(!)**

Extra Practice
See **Periods, Question Marks, and Exclamation Points** (pages CS 12–CS 13) in the back of this book.

Here's how my paper looked after I edited it.

Proofreading Marks

≡ Make a capital letter.

/ Make a small letter.

∧ Add something.

— Take out something.

⊙ Add a period.

¶ New paragraph

[DRAFT]

How to Make a Jigsaw Puzzle

_h_ave you ever made a jigsaw puzzle? I have⊙ I'll tell you how to do it. First, find a colorful picture in a magazine. Pictures of the outdoors work best. I love the outdoors. Then cut a piece of heavy paper so it's the same size as the picture. Next, paste the picture on the heavy paper. Draw two wavy lines across and two wavy lines down the back of the paper. Finally, cut the picture apart on the lines. _n_ow you have the pieces of a puzzle. Mix up the pieces. What a mess! Can you put them together again to make the picture?

Let the paste dry.

Publishing

Share

Post my how-to paper on our school's Web site.

After proofreading, I was ready to make a final copy to share with others. This is called **publishing**. Here's what I did to publish my how-to paper.

1. I copied my paper with all of my changes. I used my best handwriting. I made sure I put my name on it.

2. I asked my sister to type my how-to paper on a computer and save it on a disk.

3. I gave the disk to the computer teacher.

4. The computer teacher put my paper on the school's Web site.

5. I read my paper aloud in class. Then we all looked it up on the school's Web site.

How to Make a Jigsaw Puzzle
by Tai

Have you ever made a jigsaw puzzle? I have. I'll tell you how to do it. First, find a colorful picture in a magazine. Pictures of the outdoors work best. Then cut a piece of heavy paper so it's the same size as the picture. Next, paste the picture on the heavy paper. Let the paste dry. Draw two wavy lines across and two wavy lines down the back of the paper. Finally, cut the picture apart on the lines. Now you have the pieces of a puzzle. Mix up the pieces. What a mess! Can you put them together again to make the picture?

USING the Rubric for Assessment

Go to pages 112–113 in the **Practice the Strategy Notebook!** Use the rubric to check Tai's how-to paper.

Science

Your Own Writing

EXPOSITORY

Use what you learned in this unit to write your own report, how-to paper, or both! Try these ideas.

- Use **Your Own Writing** pages in the *Practice the Strategy Notebook*.
- Pick a topic below, and write something new.
- Choose another idea of your own.

Follow the steps in the writing process. Use the Report Rubric on pages 94–95 in the *Practice the Strategy Notebook* or the How-to Paper Rubric on pages 112–113 in the *Practice the Strategy Notebook* to check your writing.

Report
• an animal
• a planet or the moon
• a force of nature (tornado, lightning, or volcano)
• an invention

How-to Paper
• how to make a special food
• how to do a job
• how to play a game
• how to grow a plant
• how to care for a pet

portfolio

School–Home Connection

Keep a writing folder. Add **Your Own Writing** pages to your writing folder. You may want to take your writing folder home to share.

NARRATIVE

Writing to Tell a Story About Someone Else

1

Once Upon a Time Story

2

Fable

Writing a Once Upon a Time Story

Hi, my name is Jaime. I live in Colorado. I'm going to help you write a story that's a lot of fun. First, you think of a famous Once Upon a Time Story like "Cinderella" or "The Three Little Pigs." Then you write the story again in your own way! You can put in new people. You can make new things happen. This is called **writing a Once Upon a Time Story**.

First, read this Once Upon a Time Story. It's a lot like "Cinderella."

Tranh

by Carlie Whitefeather

Once upon a time, a boy named Tranh moved to a new country. He went to a new school. He couldn't speak English. No one could talk to him or play with him. Even his baseball glove didn't fit him. Tranh wanted to make friends. One day, a boy in Tranh's class decided to help Tranh. He was from Vietnam, just like Tranh. He talked and played with Tranh. He helped Tranh understand his new school, his new teachers, and the other kids. Soon, Tranh was talking and playing with the other kids. He made many new friends. Even his baseball glove fit now. Tranh lived happily ever after.

Once Upon a Time Story

Rubric

Directions: First, read each question. Then read the answers for each question. Work with a partner to give Carlie Whitefeather's Once Upon a Time Story 1, 2, or 3 stars on each question.

A rubric can help you decide if a piece of writing needs more work. We'll use this rubric to look at Carlie's Once Upon a Time Story.

Does the writer make the new story sound interesting to the reader? **Audience**

Does the story have a clear beginning, middle, and end? **Organization**

Does the story have enough action verbs? **Elaboration**

Does every sentence fit the story? **Clarification**

Does every proper noun begin with a capital letter?

The story doesn't sound very interesting to the reader.

The story sounds fairly interesting to the reader.

The story sounds very interesting to the reader.

The story has a clear beginning, but the middle and end are not clear.

The story has a clear beginning and end, but events in the middle are not very clear.

The story has a clear beginning, middle, and end.

The story has very few action verbs.

The story has some action verbs.

The story has many action verbs.

Some sentences fit the story.

Most sentences fit the story.

All of the sentences fit the story.

Some proper nouns begin with a capital letter.

Most proper nouns begin with a capital letter.

All proper nouns begin with a capital letter.

Using the
Rubric

Directions: Jaime and his writing partner, Marcus, used the rubric to check Carlie Whitefeather's story. Read what they decided.

Does the writer make the new story sound interesting to the reader?

Marcus and I thought that Carlie wrote a very interesting story. It's a lot like "Cinderella", but Carlie's story seems more real. It sounds like a story a kid my age would write. That made it interesting to me! Cinderella had help from her fairy godmother. Tranh had help, too. Here's who helped him.

One day, a boy in Tranh's class decided to help Tranh.

Does the story have a clear beginning, middle, and end?

The new story has a clear beginning, middle, and end. The beginning introduces Tranh. The middle of the story tells what happens. The end of the story tells how everything turns out.

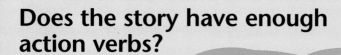

Tranh lived happily ever after.

Does the story have enough action verbs?

The new story has lots of action verbs! Action verbs tell what someone does. This sentence has two action verbs. Can you find them?

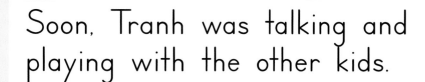

Soon, Tranh was talking and playing with the other kids.

Does every sentence fit the story?

Every sentence in the story is about Tranh or about something that happens to him. Here are some more sentences about Tranh.

No one could talk to him or play with him. Even his baseball glove didn't fit him.

Does every proper noun begin with a capital letter?

Every word that tells the name of a person, place, or thing begins with a capital letter. In this sentence, **Vietnam** and **Tranh** are proper nouns. They begin with a capital letter because one is a country's name and the other is a person's name.

He was from Vietnam, just like Tranh.

I'm a writer, too! Now I'm going to rewrite a Once Upon a Time Story. Read to see how I do it.

Jaime

Name: Jaime
Home: Colorado
Hobbies: reading, building models
Favorite Subject: social studies
Favorite Book: *Just So Stories* by Rudyard Kipling
Assignment: rewrite a Once Upon a Time Story

Gather Ideas

Decide which story to rewrite. Make notes about the story.

My favorite Once Upon a Time Story is "The Three Little Pigs." I'm going to rewrite it. I'm going to change it a lot!

I'm starting my story by **prewriting,** or planning. I'm going to make notes to change the characters and change what happens.

I want to keep the pigs and the wolf in my story. I'll change a lot about them, though. I'll make the pigs skinny and poor. I'll change what happens to them. I'll change the wolf, too. Look at my notes on the next page.

My Once Upon a Time Story

The Three Poor Little Pigs

My Notes

- three little pigs
- the wolf didn't visit them
- poor
- were in a straw house
- rich uncle gave them a present
- got three big bags of money
- built a brick house
- pigs were rich
- shared their home and food

Stop! and Go! Try this yourself on page 114 in the **Practice** the Strategy **Notebook!**

Prewriting
Organize

Make a story map to tell who is in the story and what happens.

The next step was to **organize** my notes. That means putting everything where it belongs. I talked with my writing partner, Marcus. We thought that a **story map** would be a great way to organize my notes.

Story Map

A **story map** organizes a story into a beginning, a middle, and an end. The beginning tells the characters and the problem. The middle tells what happens. The end tells how the problem is fixed.

I put my notes in the story map. First, I told the characters and the beginning of the story. Then I told the middle. Then I told the end of the story. Look at my story map on the next page.

My Story: The Three Poor Little Pigs

Beginning

three little pigs

poor

were in a straw house

the wolf didn't visit them

Middle

rich uncle gave them a present

got three big bags of money

pigs were rich

End

built a brick house

shared their home and food

Read Jaime's story map again. Do you think it organizes his story into a beginning, a middle, and an end? Talk about Jaime's story map with a partner.

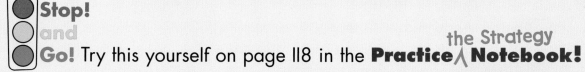

Stop! and Go! Try this yourself on page II8 in the **Practice the Strategy Notebook!**

Drafting

Write

Use my story map. Write sentences to tell what happens at the beginning, middle, and end.

Now, I was ready to **draft**, or write, my story. I used my story map to write sentences. I made sure that I told what happened at the beginning, in the middle, and at the end of my story.

I didn't worry too much about making mistakes, though. I can fix them later. Look at my draft on the next page.

The Three Poor Little Pigs [DRAFT]

Once upon a time, there were three little pigs. That's my favorite Once Upon a Time Story. They were poor. They were in a straw house. They had no food. Even william goodwolf did not visit them. One day a letter from uncle pigtail was in the mail. He gave the pigs a present. They got three big bags of money. Suddenly, the pigs were rich! Cinderella was very poor and then became rich, too. After that, the pigs had a brick house. They were never hungry again. They shared their home and food. They even invited william goodwolf to dinner once a week.

ORAL LANGUAGE
Talk With a Partner
COOPERATIVE LEARNING

Talk with a partner about Jaime's draft. Do you think it has a good beginning, middle, and end? Tell why or why not.

Stop!
and
Go! Try this yourself on page 122 in the *Practice* ∧ *Notebook*! the Strategy

Revising

Add (Elaborate)

Add action verbs to make the story more exciting.

Next it was time to **revise** my story. When I revise, I make my writing even better. The rubric says my story should have **action verbs**. Action verbs tell what people do. It's a lot more fun to read about people doing things than just hanging around.

I know that **is, are, was,** and **were** are not action verbs. Those verbs don't make my story exciting! I changed some of them to action verbs. Look at my changes on the next page.

Action Verbs

Action verbs tell what someone is doing or already did. Here are some action verbs.

goes	talks
jumps	plays
sleeps	eats

The Three Poor Little Pigs

Once upon a time, there were three little pigs. That's my favorite Once Upon a Time Story. They were poor. They ~~were~~ *lived* in a straw house. They had no food. Even william goodwolf did not visit them. One day a letter from uncle pigtail ~~was~~ *came* in the mail. He gave the pigs a present. They got three big bags of money. Suddenly, the pigs were rich! Cinderella was very poor and then became rich, too. After that, the pigs ~~had~~ *built* a brick house. They were never hungry again. They shared their home and food. They even invited william goodwolf to dinner once a week.

Can you think of other ways to make Jaime's draft better? Talk with a partner about your ideas.

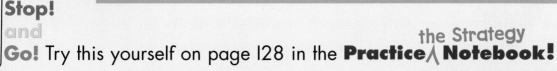

Stop! and Go! Try this yourself on page 128 in the **Practice the Strategy Notebook!**

Revising

Take Out
(Clarify)

Take out sentences that don't fit the story.

Next, I talked to my writing partner, Marcus, again. Marcus and I read each other's stories and think of ways to make them better. Marcus reminded me that the rubric says that all my sentences should fit the story. Marcus found two sentences that didn't fit! I crossed out those two sentences. Here's how my story looks now.

The Three Poor Little Pigs

~~lived~~

Once upon a time, there were three little pigs. ~~That's my favorite Once Upon a Time Story.~~ They were poor. They ~~were~~ in a straw house. They had no food. Even william goodwolf did not visit them. One day a letter from uncle pigtail ~~was~~ in the mail. He gave the pigs a present. They got three big bags of money. Suddenly, the pigs were rich! ~~Cinderella was very poor and then became rich, too.~~ After that, the pigs ~~had~~ a brick house. They were never hungry again. They shared their home and food. They even invited william goodwolf to dinner once a week.

lived

came

built

Editing
Proofread

Make sure I begin every proper noun with a capital letter.

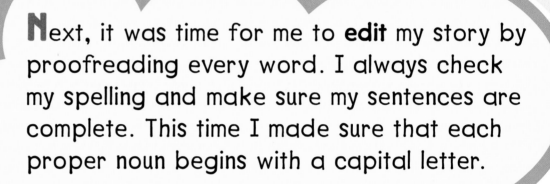

Next, it was time for me to **edit** my story by proofreading every word. I always check my spelling and make sure my sentences are complete. This time I made sure that each proper noun begins with a capital letter.

Proper Nouns

A **proper noun** is the name of a person, place, or thing. A proper noun begins with a capital letter.

Person: Jill Smith, Grandpa Joe, Mr. Jones

Place: New Jersey, Hudson River, Main Street

Thing: Tuesday, June, Thanksgiving

Extra Practice
See **Proper Nouns**
(pages CS 14-CS 15) in the back of this book.

Here's how my story looks after I edited it.

[DRAFT]

The Three Poor Little Pigs

Once upon a time, there were three little pigs. ~~That's my favorite Once Upon a Time Story.~~ They were poor. They ~~were~~ *lived* in a straw house. They had no food. Even ~~w~~illiam ~~g~~oodwolf did not visit them. One day a letter from ~~u~~ncle ~~p~~igtail ~~was~~ *came* in the mail. He gave the pigs a present. They got three big bags of money. Suddenly, the pigs were rich! ~~Cinderella was very poor and then became rich, too.~~ After that, the pigs ~~had~~ *built* a brick house. They were never hungry again. They shared their home and food. They even invited ~~w~~illiam ~~g~~oodwolf to dinner once a week.

Stop!
and
Go! Try this yourself on page 130 in the **Practice** the Strategy **Notebook!**

Publishing
Share

Post my Once Upon a Time Story on our class bulletin board.

After I edited my story, I made a neat final copy to **publish** it. That means sharing my story with others. My teacher put everyone's story on our class bulletin board. Now all of us can read every Once Upon a Time Story! Here's what I did to publish my story.

1. I copied my story in my best handwriting. I made all my changes and added my name.

2. I pasted my story onto a big sheet of red paper. That gave my story a cool looking border.

3. I gave my story to my teacher for our class bulletin board.

The Three Poor Little Pigs
by Jaime

Once upon a time, there were three little pigs. They were poor. They lived in a straw house. They had no food. Even William Goodwolf did not visit them. One day a letter from Uncle Pigtail arrived in the mail. He gave the pigs a present. They got three big bags of money. Suddenly, the pigs were rich! After that, the pigs built a brick house. They were never hungry again. They shared their home and food. They even invited William Goodwolf to dinner once a week.

USING the Rubric for Assessment

Go to page 132 in the **Practice** the Strategy **Notebook!** Use the rubric to check Jaime's Once Upon a Time Story.

Writing a
Fable

Hi, my name is Mina. I live in Washington, D.C. I'm going to help you write a **fable**. I'm going to write my favorite fable in my own way. I will put in new characters. I will change the events, too. This is called **writing a fable**.

Do you know the fable about a lion and a mouse? The lion saves the mouse's life. The mouse promises to help the lion. The big lion laughs, but one day the mouse helps the lion! The lesson is this—even someone tiny can help someone big and strong.

Fable

A **fable** is a story that teaches a lesson. Sometimes, the last sentence of the fable explains the lesson. In a fable, animals often talk and act like humans.

First, read this fable. It's a lot like the fable about the lion and the mouse.

MODEL
FABLE

Lily and the Firefighter
by Chad Haziz

One day, little Lily was playing with a ball. The ball got stuck on Ms. Ramos's roof.

Ms. Ramos said, "Don't worry, Lily. I'll get the ball for you."

Lily said, "I will help you one day, Ms. Ramos."

Ms. Ramos laughed. How could a small, quiet girl like Lily help her? Ms. Ramos was a brave, strong firefighter. A year later, an empty house on Lily's street was on fire. Lily knew what to do! She ran to Ms. Ramos. Lily told her there was a puppy in that house. Ms. Ramos went straight to that room. She saved the puppy! Quiet little Lily turned out to be a big help after all.

Fable

Rubric

Directions: First, read each question. Then read the answers for each question. Work with a partner to give Chad Haziz's fable 1, 2, or 3 stars on each question.

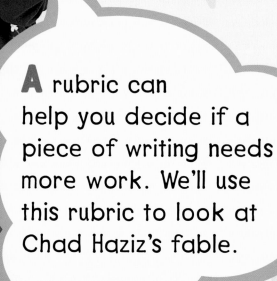

A rubric can help you decide if a piece of writing needs more work. We'll use this rubric to look at Chad Haziz's fable.

Does the new fable sound right to the reader? Is it like the famous fable?

Audience

Does the fable tell the characters at the beginning, the story in the middle, and the lesson at the end?

Organization

Does the fable have enough describing words to make the characters seem real?

Elaboration

Does every sentence belong in the fable?

Clarification

Are quotation marks used correctly?

conventions & Skills

★

The fable doesn't sound right. It's nothing like the famous fable.

The fable tells the characters at the beginning, but the story is mixed up, and there's no lesson.

The fable has very few describing words. The characters don't seem real.

Some of the sentences belong in the fable.

Some quotation marks are used correctly.

★★

The fable mostly sounds right, but it's still different from the famous fable.

The fable tells the characters at the beginning and the story in the middle, but it needs a lesson.

The fable has some describing words to make the characters seem real.

Most of the sentences belong in the fable.

Most quotation marks are used correctly.

★★★

The fable sounds right to the reader. It's new, but it's a lot like the famous fable.

The fable tells the characters at the beginning, the story in the middle, and the lesson at the end.

The fable has many describing words to make the characters seem real.

All of the sentences belong in the fable.

All quotation marks are used correctly.

Using the Rubric

Directions: Mina and her writing partner, Victoria, used the rubric to check Chad's fable. Read what they decided.

Does the new fable sound right to the reader? Is it like the famous fable?

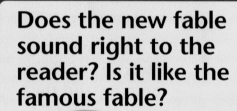

Victoria and I thought that this fable sounded right. It's new, but it's a lot like "The Lion and the Mouse." A quiet little girl helps a strong grown-up firefighter just like the weak little mouse helps the big, strong lion. The end of the fable tells the same lesson as the famous fable.

Quiet little Lily turned out to be a big help after all.

Does the fable tell the characters at the beginning, the story in the middle, and the lesson at the end?

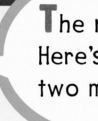

The new fable does all of these things. Here's the beginning. It introduces the two main characters, Lily and Ms. Ramos.

One day, little Lily was playing with a ball. The ball got stuck on Ms. Ramos's roof.

Does the fable have enough describing words to make the characters seem real?

The new fable has lots of describing words that tell about the characters. Look at this sentence. It uses two describing words to make Ms. Ramos more real. Can you find them?

Ms. Ramos was a brave, strong firefighter.

Does every sentence belong in the fable?

Every sentence in the fable is about Lily or Ms. Ramos and what happens to them. This sentence is an example.

About a year later, an empty house on Lily's street was on fire.

Are quotation marks used correctly?

Quotation marks (" ") go at the beginning and at the end of what someone says. In this sentence, the words that Lily says are in quotation marks.

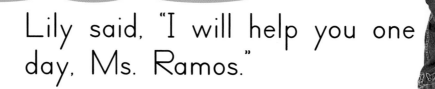

Lily said, "I will help you one day, Ms. Ramos."

I'm a writer, too! Now, I'm going to rewrite my favorite fable. It's going to be lots of fun! Read to see how I do it.

Name: Mina
Home: Washington, D.C.
Hobbies: riding a bike, playing the violin
Favorite Book: *Harold and the Purple Crayon* by Crockett Johnson
Assignment: retell a fable

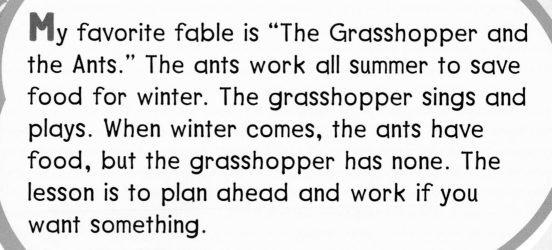

Decide which fable to rewrite. Make notes about the fable.

My favorite fable is "The Grasshopper and the Ants." The ants work all summer to save food for winter. The grasshopper sings and plays. When winter comes, the ants have food, but the grasshopper has none. The lesson is to plan ahead and work if you want something.

I'm going to rewrite this fable. I'll change the animals to people. I'll make the story happen now! The first thing I need to do is **prewrite,** or plan my story. First, I'll make notes about the fable. Look at my notes on the next page.

My Fable

Jen and Jule

want to go to water park

parents will take them if they earn money

My Notes

Jen	Jule
like the ants	like the grasshopper
saves allowance	spends allowance
does special jobs for pay	doesn't do anything extra
has money for water park	has no money for water park

Lesson—Plan ahead and work hard if you want something.

Stop! and Go! Try this yourself on page 134 in the **Practice** the Strategy **Notebook!**

Make a story map to tell who is in the fable and what happens.

After I had my notes, I put my notes in a story map. The story map helped me organize my ideas! Here's how I put my notes in my story map. First, I told who the characters were and what happened at the beginning. Next, I told what happened in the middle. The last thing I told is the lesson my fable teaches. Look at my story map on the next page.

My Fable: Jen and Jule

Beginning

Characters—Jen and Jule

Problem—need money for water park

Middle

Jen—saves money

does special jobs for pay

Jule—spends money

doesn't do anything extra

End

Jen—has money to go

Jule—has no money to go

Lesson—Plan ahead and work

hard if you want something.

Find a partner and read Mina's story map together. Do you think it helps organize her ideas for her fable? Talk about Mina's story map with your partner.

Stop!
and
Go! Try this yourself on page 138 in the **Practice** the Strategy **Notebook!**

Drafting
Write

Use my story map. Write sentences to tell what happens at the beginning, middle, and end.

Now I was ready to **draft,** or write my fable. I used my story map to write sentences. I made sure to write sentences about the characters at the beginning. Then I wrote sentences to tell what happened in the middle. Finally, I wrote the end of my fable and the lesson.

Jen and Jule

Jen and Jule wanted to go to Wet World Water Park. They live on Oak Street.

Their parents said, We don't have much extra money this month. If you can pay to get in, we will take you.

Every week, Jen saved money. She did special jobs for pay. Jen likes math a lot. Jule spent all her money on snacks. She was going to sell lemonade. She never did it. At the end of the month, Jen had money for Wet World.

I'm ready to go! she said.

Jule had nothing but empty snack boxes. If you need money, you have to plan ahead, work hard, and save!

Talk with a partner about Mina's draft. Do you think her fable has a beginning, a middle, and an end? Find each part.

Stop!
and
Go! Try this yourself on page 142 in the **Practice ∧ Notebook!**
the Strategy

Narrative Writing • Fable   183

Revising
Add
(Elaborate)

Add describing words to make the characters more real.

Now I was ready to **revise** my writing. I wanted to make my fable even better. One way to do that is to use describing words to tell even more about the **characters**.

I used sticky notes to add describing words. My new describing words helped make my characters more real for my reader! Look at my changes on the next page.

Characters

Characters are the people or animals in a story. In a fable, the characters are often animals, who talk and act like people.

Jen and Jule

Jen and Jule wanted to go to Wet World Water Park. They live on Oak Street.

Their parents said, We don't have much extra money this month. If you can pay to get in, we will take you.

smart

Every week, Jen saved money. She did special jobs for pay. Jen likes math a lot. Jule spent all her money on snacks. She was going to sell lemonade. She never did it. At the end of the month, Jen had money for Wet World.

Silly

happy

I'm ready to go! she said.

Sad

Jule had nothing but empty snack boxes. If you need money, you have to plan ahead, work hard, and save!

ORAL LANGUAGE
Talk With a **Partner**
COOPERATIVE LEARNING

Can you think of other ways to make Mina's draft better? Talk with a partner about your ideas.

Stop! and Go! Try this yourself on page 146 in the **Practice** the Strategy **Notebook!**

Revising
Take Out
(Clarify)

Take out sentences that make the fable confusing.

Next, I read my fable to Victoria, my writing partner. We always read our writing to each other to help make it even better. Victoria found two sentences that confused her. She didn't understand why I included where Jen and Jule live. She also didn't understand why I said that Jen likes math.

She was right! Those sentences just made the fable confusing. I crossed them out. Here's how my paper looks now.

[DRAFT]

Jen and Jule

Jen and Jule wanted to go to Wet World Water Park. ~~They live on Oak Street.~~

Their parents said, We don't have much extra money this month. If you can pay to get in, we will take you.

Every week, Jen saved money. She did special jobs for pay. ~~Jen likes math a lot.~~ Jule spent all her money on snacks. She was going to sell lemonade. She never did it. At the end of the month, Jen had money for Wet World.

I'm ready to go! she said.

Jule had nothing but empty snack boxes. If you need money, you have to plan ahead, work hard, and save!

smart

Silly

happy

Sad

Stop!
and
Go! Try this yourself on page 147 in the **Practice** the Strategy **Notebook!**

Proofread

Make sure I use quotation marks correctly.

Now it was time to **edit** my fable by proofreading every word. I always check my spelling, my sentences, and my punctuation. This time, I wanted to make sure that I used quotation marks correctly.

Quotation Marks

Use **quotation marks** (" ") to show where the words someone says begin and where they end.

- The lion said, "You cannot help me."

- "A mouse can sometimes help a lion," the mouse answered.

Extra Practice
See **Quotation Marks** (pages CS 16–CS 17) in the back of this book.

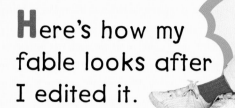

Here's how my fable looks after I edited it.

[DRAFT]

Jen and Jule

Jen and Jule wanted to go to Wet World Water Park. They live on Oak Street.

Their parents said, "We don't have much extra money this month. If you can pay to get in, we will take you."

Every week, Jen saved money. She did special jobs for pay. ~~Jen likes math a lot.~~ Jule spent all her money on snacks. She was going to sell lemonade. She never did it. At the end of the month, Jen had money for Wet World. "I'm ready to go!" she said.

Jule had nothing but empty snack boxes. If you need money, you have to plan ahead, work hard, and save!

 smart

 Silly

happy

 Sad

Stop!
and
Go! Try this yourself on page 148 in the **Practice** the Strategy ∧ **Notebook!**

Publishing
Share

Draw a picture to go with my fable. Put fables together to make a class book.

Now I was ready to share my fable by **publishing** it. I read my new fable aloud to share it with the kids in my class. Then I listened to the other kids read their fables, too. Here's what else I did to publish my fable.

1. I made a final copy of my fable by including all my changes. I used my best handwriting. I also added my name.

2. I drew some pictures to go with my fable.

3. My teacher put all the fables into a class book. It will go into our class library.

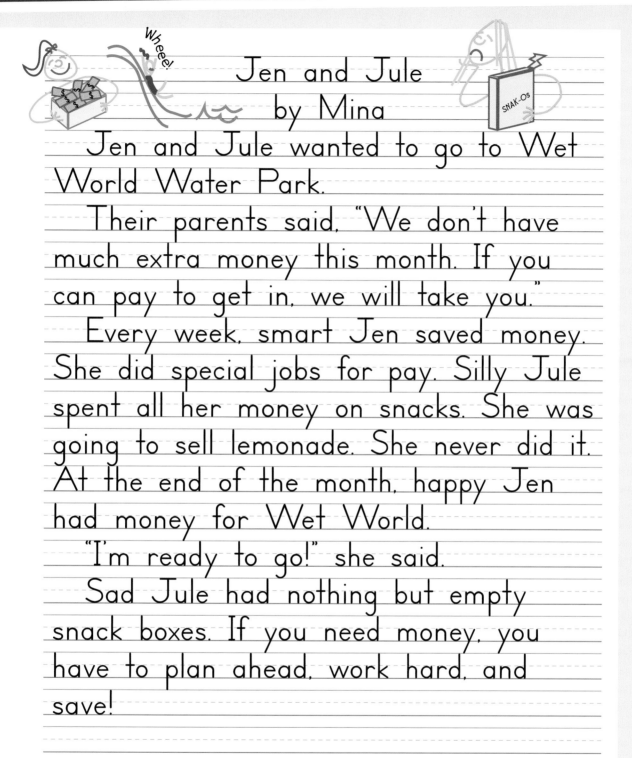

Jen and Jule
by Mina

Jen and Jule wanted to go to Wet World Water Park.

Their parents said, "We don't have much extra money this month. If you can pay to get in, we will take you."

Every week, smart Jen saved money. She did special jobs for pay. Silly Jule spent all her money on snacks. She was going to sell lemonade. She never did it. At the end of the month, happy Jen had money for Wet World.

"I'm ready to go!" she said.

Sad Jule had nothing but empty snack boxes. If you need money, you have to plan ahead, work hard, and save!

USING the Rubric for Assessment

Go to page 150 in the **Practice the Strategy Notebook!** Use the rubric to check Mina's fable.

Responding to Literature
Your Own Writing
NARRATIVE

Use what you learned in this unit to rewrite your own Once Upon a Time Story, fable, or both! Try these ideas.

- Use **Your Own Writing** pages in the *Practice the Strategy Notebook*.
- Pick a topic below, and write something new.
- Choose another idea of your own.

Follow the steps in the writing process. Use the Once Upon a Time Story Rubric on pages 132–133 in the *Practice the Strategy Notebook* or the Fable Rubric on pages 150–151 in the *Practice the Strategy Notebook* to check your writing.

Once Upon a Time Story	Fable

- "The Elves and the Shoemaker"
- "Three Billy Goats Gruff"
- "Rumpelstiltskin"
- "Stone Soup"

- "The Tortoise and the Hare"
- "The Fox and the Crow"
- "The City Mouse and the Country Mouse"
- "The North Wind and the Sun"

portfolio

School–Home Connection

Keep a writing folder. Add **Your Own Writing** pages to your writing folder. You may want to take your writing folder home to share.

PERSUASIVE

Writing to Tell What I Think

1

Opinion Paper

2

Opinion Speech

Writing an Opinion Paper

Hi, my name is Nicole. I live in Utah. If you're like me, you have **opinions** about all kinds of things. I'll help you share what you think in writing. This kind of writing is called an **opinion paper**.

Opinion

An **opinion** tells what a person thinks or feels about something.

First, read this opinion paper. It's a good model.

My Favorite Meal
by Mitch Muller

My favorite meal is tomato soup. One reason I like it so much is that it is simple to make. You just open a can. You pour the soup into a bowl. Then you can heat the soup in a microwave.

Tomato soup goes with almost everything. You can eat it with crackers or toast. It tastes great with most sandwiches.

Best of all, tomato soup warms you up on a cold day. You can warm your hands. Just hold the cup or the bowl. Tomato soup warms up your insides, too. For a great meal, you just can't beat tomato soup.

Opinion Paper

Rubric

Directions: First, read each question. Then read the answers for each question. Work with a partner to give Mitch Muller's opinion paper 1, 2, or 3 stars on each question.

A rubric can help you decide if a piece of writing needs more work. We'll use this rubric to look at Mitch Muller's opinion paper.

Does the paper clearly state the writer's opinion for the reader? **Audience**

Is there one paragraph for each reason? **Organization**

Are there enough details to explain each reason? **Elaboration**

Does every sentence help explain the writer's opinion? **Clarification**

Does every sentence have a subject and a predicate? **conventions & Skills**

★

The paper doesn't state the writer's opinion for the reader.

There is only one paragraph for all the reasons.

There are few details to explain the reasons.

Some of the sentences help explain the writer's opinion.

Some sentences have a subject and a predicate.

★★

The paper states the writer's opinion for the reader, but it's not clear.

There are two paragraphs, but the reasons are all mixed up.

There are some details to explain the reasons.

Most of the sentences help explain the writer's opinion.

Most sentences have a subject and a predicate.

★★★

The paper clearly states the writer's opinion for the reader.

There is one paragraph for each reason.

There are many details to explain all of the reasons.

All of the sentences help explain the writer's opinion.

All sentences have a subject and a predicate.

Using the
Rubric

Does the paper clearly state the writer's opinion?

Sierra and I looked for the writer's opinion in the opinion paper. This paper starts out right! The opinion is in the first sentence.

My favorite meal is tomato soup.

Is there one paragraph for each reason?

We found three paragraphs. Each paragraph tells about one reason. Here's the second sentence of the first paragraph. It tells the first reason.

One reason I like it so much is that it is simple to make.

Are there enough details to explain each reason?

Every reason has lots of details to explain it. Read these details. They explain why tomato soup is simple to make.

You just open a can. You pour the soup into a bowl. Then you can heat the soup in a microwave.

Does every sentence help explain the writer's opinion?

Every sentence helps explain why tomato soup is the writer's favorite meal. Read these sentences.

You can eat it with crackers or toast. It tastes great with most sandwiches.

Does every sentence have a subject and a predicate?

The subject of a sentence tells who or what does something. The predicate tells what the subject does or is. All the sentences in this opinion paper have a subject and a predicate. Can you find the subject and the predicate in this sentence?

Tomato soup warms up your insides, too.

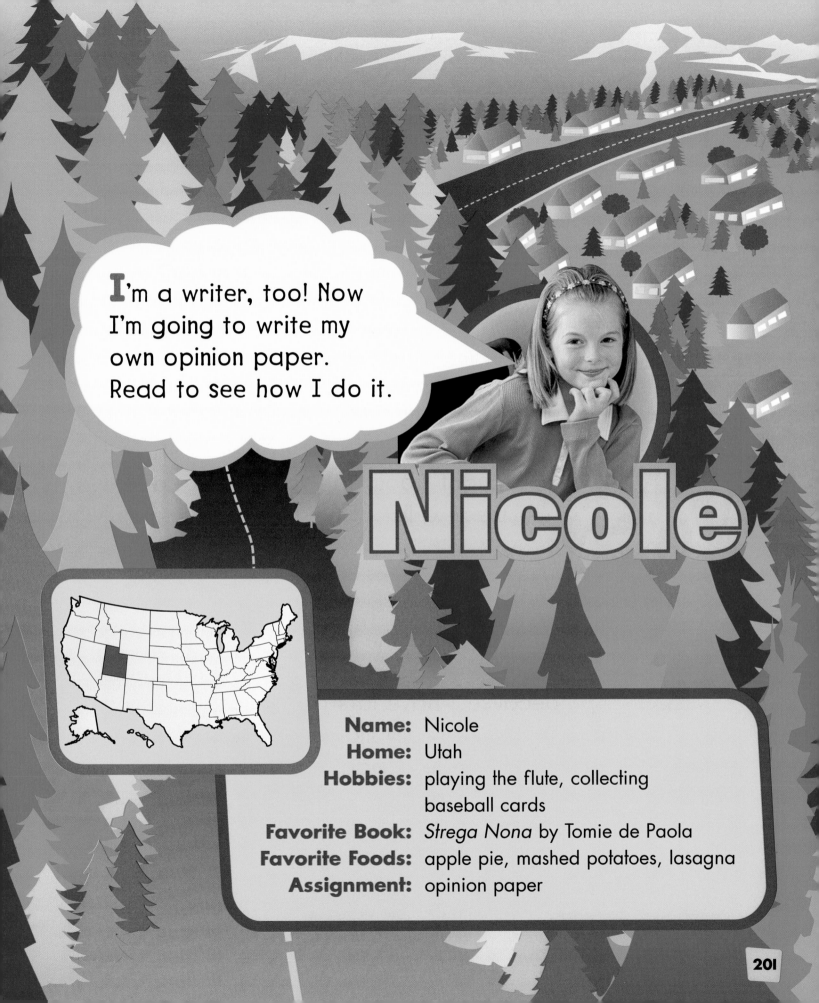

I'm a writer, too! Now I'm going to write my own opinion paper. Read to see how I do it.

Nicole

Name: Nicole
Home: Utah
Hobbies: playing the flute, collecting baseball cards
Favorite Book: *Strega Nona* by Tomie de Paola
Favorite Foods: apple pie, mashed potatoes, lasagna
Assignment: opinion paper

Prewriting

Gather Ideas

Think about foods I like. Pick one to write about.

Let me show you how I wrote my opinion paper. I started with **prewriting**. That means I did some planning before I started writing my paper. First, I thought about the foods I like a lot. I made a list of my favorites.

Then I chose the food that I think makes the best meal. I picked lasagna because I have lots of reasons for my opinion. I really like lasagna! Read my list on the next page.

Foods I Like

apple pie

mashed potatoes

lasagna

My Thinking

It tastes great, but you can't have it for your whole dinner!

They taste great. They're easy to eat.

It tastes great. It's easy to eat. It's good for you. Lasagna makes the best meal. That's my opinion. I'm going to write about lasagna!

Stop!
and
Go! Try this yourself on page 152 in the **Practice** the Strategy **Notebook!**

Prewriting
Organize

Make a spider map to organize my reasons.

Lasagna makes the best meal of any food. That's my opinion. I made a **spider map** to help me organize my opinion paper. I wrote my opinion in the middle of the spider. I wrote one reason on each leg. Then I wrote some **details** for the reasons.

I worked on my spider map with my writing partner, Sierra. Look at my spider map on the next page.

Spider Map

A **spider map** organizes ideas for a paper. Write your opinion in the middle of the "spider." Write your reasons on the spider's "legs."

Details

Details give more information. Details explain reasons and opinions.

Persuasive Writing • Opinion Paper

My Opinion: Lasagna Makes the Best Meal

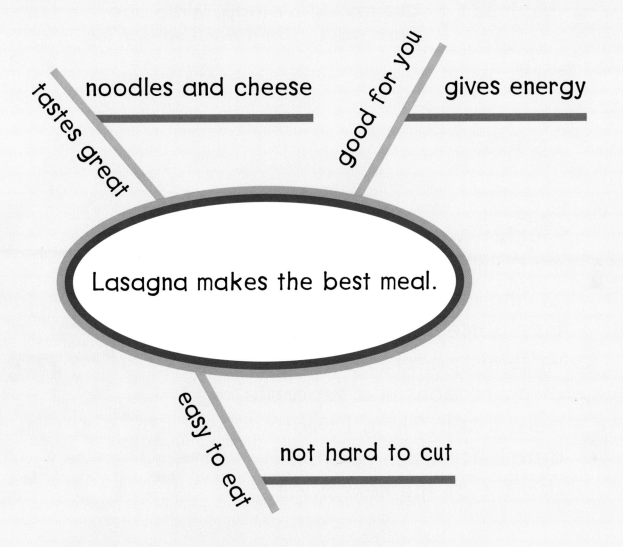

noodles and cheese

good for you

gives energy

tastes great

Lasagna makes the best meal.

easy to eat

not hard to cut

ORAL LANGUAGE

Talk
With a
Partner

COOPERATIVE LEARNING

Find a partner and read Nicole's spider map together. Do you think it tells her opinion? Does it give reasons for her opinion?

Stop!
and
Go! Try this yourself on page 156 in the **Practice** the Strategy **Notebook!**

Drafting
Write

Use my spider map. Write one paragraph about each spider leg.

Next, it was time to **draft** my opinion paper. That means writing my paper for the first time. I used my spider map to write my paper. I put each of my reasons in a separate **paragraph**. Then, I wrote details for each reason. My draft is on the next page.

Paragraph

A **paragraph** is a group of sentences. All the sentences are about the same idea. The first sentence of a paragraph is indented. That means it starts a little to the right.

The Best Meal

Lasagna is the best meal you can eat. One reason is that it tastes great. That's because it has soft noodles and melted cheese. has yummy tomato sauce, too. Mashed potatoes are almost as good.

Another reason is that lasagna is easy to eat. It isn't hard to cut. isn't hard to chew. It doesn't stick to your teeth. Peanut butter sticks to my teeth.

Another reason lasagna is the best meal is that it is good for you. Lasagna fills you up and gives you energy. Lasagna!

Talk with a partner about Nicole's draft. Does it begin with an opinion? Does it have one paragraph for each reason?

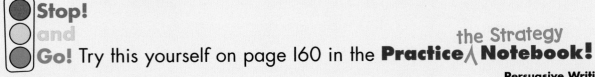

Stop! **and** **Go!** Try this yourself on page 160 in the **Practice** the Strategy **Notebook!**

Revising

Add
(Elaborate)

Add details to explain my reasons.

Next it was time to **revise**! That means changing some things to make my opinion paper even better. One way to revise is to add more details. Details can help me explain my reasons better.

I found a place where I didn't explain my reasons enough. I decided to give more details about why lasagna is good for you. I used a sticky note to add them. Look at my new details on the next page.

The Best Meal

Lasagna is the best meal you can eat. One reason is that it tastes great. That's because it has soft noodles and melted cheese. has yummy tomato sauce, too. Mashed potatoes are almost as good.

Another reason is that lasagna is easy to eat. It isn't hard to cut. isn't hard to chew. It doesn't stick to your teeth. Peanut butter sticks to my teeth.

Another reason lasagna is the best meal is that it is good for you. Lasagna fills you up and gives you energy. Lasagna!

The cheese helps build your bones. The sauce has vitamins.

Can you think of other ways to make Nicole's draft better? Talk with a partner about your ideas.

Stop!
and
Go! Try this yourself on page 164 in the **Practice** the Strategy **Notebook!**

Revising
Take Out
(Clarify)

Take out sentences that don't help explain my opinion.

Next, I talked to my writing partner, Sierra. We always talk together about our writing. We help each other make our writing as good as it can be. I read my paper aloud to Sierra. She found two sentences that didn't help explain why lasagna is the best meal.

She was right! I crossed out those two sentences. Here's how my paper looks now.

The Best Meal

Lasagna is the best meal you can eat. One reason is that it tastes great. That's because it has soft noodles and melted cheese. has yummy tomato sauce, too. ~~Mashed potatoes are almost as good.~~

Another reason is that lasagna is easy to eat. It isn't hard to cut. isn't hard to chew. It doesn't stick to your teeth. ~~Peanut butter sticks to my teeth.~~

Another reason lasagna is the best meal is that it is good for you. Lasagna fills you up and gives you energy. Lasagna!

> The cheese helps build your bones. The sauce has vitamins.

Stop!
and
Go! Try this yourself on page 165 in the **Practice** the Strategy **Notebook!**

Editing

Proofread
Make sure every sentence has a subject and a predicate.

Next, I **edited** my paper. That means I proofread every word and fixed any mistakes I found. I always check my spelling and look for other problems. This time I checked that every sentence in my opinion paper has a subject and a predicate.

Subjects and Predicates

The **subject** of a sentence tells who or what does or is something. The **predicate** tells what the subject does or is.

Subject	Predicate
My mother	makes rice and beans a lot.
My favorite meal	is rice and beans!

Extra Practice
See **Subjects and Predicates** (pages CS 18–CS 19) in the back of this book.

Here's how my paper looks after I edited it.

[DRAFT]

The Best Meal

Lasagna is the best meal you can eat. One reason is that it tastes great. That's because it has soft noodles and melted cheese. ~~It~~ has yummy tomato sauce, too. ~~Mashed potatoes are almost as good.~~

Lasagna

Another reason is that lasagna is easy to eat. It isn't hard to cut. ~~It~~ isn't hard to chew. It doesn't stick to your teeth. ~~Peanut butter sticks to my teeth.~~

It

Another reason lasagna is the best meal is that it is good for you. Lasagna fills you up and gives you energy. Lasagna ~~!~~

The cheese helps build your bones. The sauce has vitamins.

is the best meal of all

Publishing

Share

Post my paper on a "Class Opinions" bulletin board.

The last step in the writing process is **publishing**. Publishing is sharing your writing with others. My teacher made a "Class Opinions" bulletin board for our opinion papers. All of us will be able to read every paper! Here's what I did to publish my paper.

1. I used my best handwriting to copy my paper. I put in all the changes I made when I revised and edited it.

2. I wrote my name under the title of my paper.

3. I gave my opinion paper to my teacher to put on our "Class Opinions" bulletin board.

The Best Meal
by Nicole

Lasagna is the best meal you can eat. One reason is that it tastes great. That's because it has soft noodles and melted cheese. Lasagna has yummy tomato sauce, too.

Another reason is that lasagna is easy to eat. It isn't hard to cut. It isn't hard to chew. It doesn't stick to your teeth.

Another reason lasagna is the best meal is that it is good for you. The cheese helps build your bones. The sauce has vitamins. Lasagna fills you up and gives you energy. Lasagna is the best meal of all!

USING the Rubric for Assessment

Go to page 168 in the **Practice the Strategy Notebook!** Use the rubric to check Nicole's opinion paper.

Writing an
Opinion Speech

Hi, my name is Jonathan. I live in Arizona. Have you ever wanted to change something? I'm going to help you write about something you want to change. First, you'll write what you think. Then, you can read it aloud to people. This kind of writing is called an **opinion speech**.

First, read this opinion speech. It's a good model.

MODEL
OPINION SPEECH

Computers in Our Library
by Courtney Lowell

We need more computers in our library. Then we could spend more time writing on the computer. Now, we can write for only ten minutes at a time. That is not enough!

With more computers, we could use the Internet more. Right now, we can't look up things when we need to. Sometimes we have to wait hours or even days.

With more computers, we could learn more computer skills. Today, some of us still don't know how to use a search engine. We could learn if we had more computers. We need more computers for all these reasons!

Opinion Speech

Rubric

Directions: First read each question. Then read the answers for each question. Work with a partner to give Courtney Lowell's opinion speech 1, 2, or 3 stars on each question.

A rubric can help you decide if a piece of writing needs more work. We'll use this rubric to look at Courtney Lowell's opinion speech.

Does the speech clearly tell the writer's opinion?

Audience

Is there one paragraph for each reason?

Organization

Are there enough facts to explain the reasons?

Elaboration

Does every sentence help explain the writer's opinion?

Clarification

Does every sentence have a subject and a predicate?

conventions & Skills

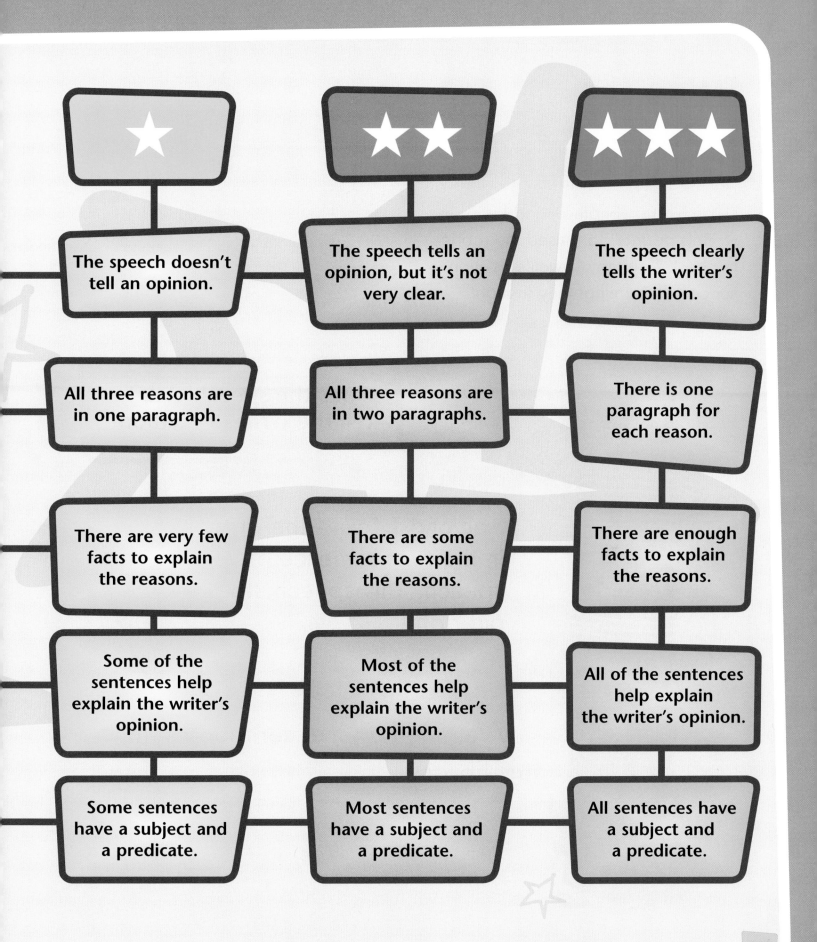

★

The speech doesn't tell an opinion.

All three reasons are in one paragraph.

There are very few facts to explain the reasons.

Some of the sentences help explain the writer's opinion.

Some sentences have a subject and a predicate.

★★

The speech tells an opinion, but it's not very clear.

All three reasons are in two paragraphs.

There are some facts to explain the reasons.

Most of the sentences help explain the writer's opinion.

Most sentences have a subject and a predicate.

★★★

The speech clearly tells the writer's opinion.

There is one paragraph for each reason.

There are enough facts to explain the reasons.

All of the sentences help explain the writer's opinion.

All sentences have a subject and a predicate.

Using the Rubric

Directions: Jonathan and his writing partner, Ian, used the rubric to check Courtney Lowell's opinion speech. Read what they thought.

Does the speech clearly tell the writer's opinion?

Ian and I found the opinion in the first sentence of the speech. This speech starts out right!

We need more computers in our library.

Is there one paragraph for each reason?

Every paragraph gives a different reason. The first paragraph gives the first reason—more time to write on the computer. The second paragraph gives the second reason—using the Internet more. The last paragraph gives this reason.

With more computers, we could learn more computer skills.

Are there enough facts to explain the reasons?

We found lots of facts to explain every reason. Here is a fact that goes with the last reason.

Today, some of us still don't know how to use a search engine.

Does every sentence help explain the writer's opinion?

All the sentences explain why the class needs more computers. These sentences explain that the students need more time to write on the computer.

Now, we can write for only ten minutes at a time. That is not enough!

Does every sentence have a subject and a predicate?

Every sentence has a subject and a predicate. The predicate tells the action. It has the verb in it. In this sentence the complete predicate is **need more computers for all these reasons!** The subject tells who does the action. Can you find the subject?

We need more computers for all these reasons!

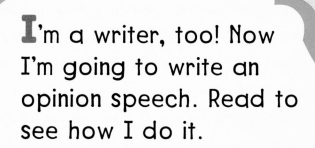

I'm a writer, too! Now I'm going to write an opinion speech. Read to see how I do it.

Jonathan

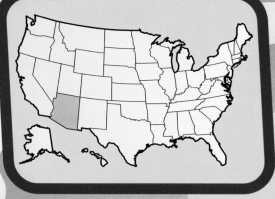

Name: Jonathan
Home: Arizona
Hobbies: playing piano, karate
Favorite Book: *My Father's Dragon* by Ruth Stiles Gannett
Favorite Sports: running, basketball
Assignment: opinion speech

Prewriting

Gather Ideas

Think about my opinions on different topics. Write some reasons for my opinions. Choose a topic.

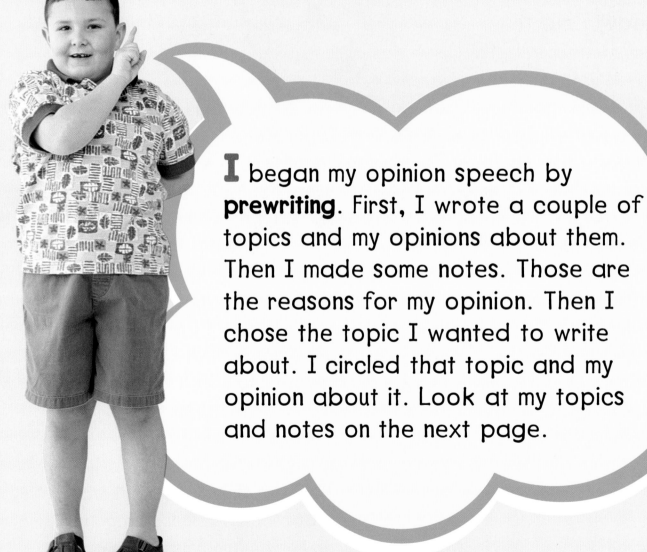

I began my opinion speech by **prewriting**. First, I wrote a couple of topics and my opinions about them. Then I made some notes. Those are the reasons for my opinion. Then I chose the topic I wanted to write about. I circled that topic and my opinion about it. Look at my topics and notes on the next page.

My Topics

school bus

playground

My Opinions and Reasons

My Opinion: It should have seat belts.

My Reason: It would be safer.

I don't have enough facts about this topic. I won't use this one.

My Opinion: Let's fix it up!

My Reasons: The swings are in bad shape.
The basketball court isn't safe.
The slide is bad.

This is great! I have lots of facts about this one. I'll use this topic for my opinion speech.

Stop!
and
Go! Try this yourself on page 170 in the **Practice** the Strategy **Notebook!**

Prewriting
Organize

Make a spider map to organize facts for my reasons.

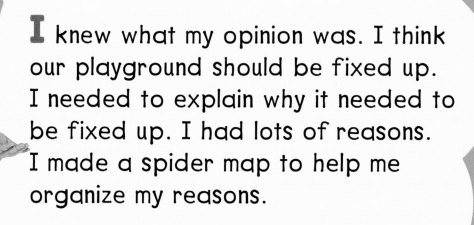

I knew what my opinion was. I think our playground should be fixed up. I needed to explain why it needed to be fixed up. I had lots of reasons. I made a spider map to help me organize my reasons.

I put my opinion in the middle of the spider. I put one reason on each of the spider's legs. Then I wrote one note for each reason to help me get started. Look at my spider map on the next page.

My Opinion: Let's Fix Up Our Playground!

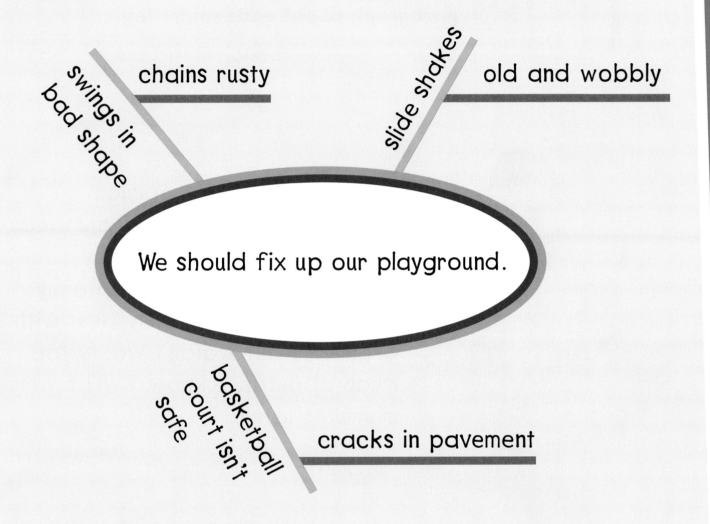

swings in bad shape

chains rusty

slide shakes

old and wobbly

We should fix up our playground.

basketball court isn't safe

cracks in pavement

ORAL LANGUAGE

Talk
With a
Partner

COOPERATIVE LEARNING

Find a partner. Read Jonathan's spider map together. What reasons does it give for his opinion? What facts explain his reasons? Talk with your partner about it.

Stop!
and
Go! Try this yourself on page 174 in the **Practice** the Strategy **Notebook!**

Drafting
Write

Use my spider map. Write one paragraph about each spider leg.

Next I drafted my opinion speech by writing out all my ideas for the first time. I used my spider map to help me write my ideas in order. I did my best with grammar, but I didn't worry too much about it. I know I will fix my mistakes later.

I wrote my opinion first. Then I wrote my first reason in the first paragraph. I wrote my second reason in my second paragraph. I wrote my third reason in my third paragraph. Read my draft on the next page.

Let's Fix Up Our Playground!

We should fix up our playground. One reason is that the swings are in bad shape. The chains The swings look terrible.

The second reason we should fix up the playground is that the slide is old and wobbly. It shakes when you climb it. Nobody wants to use it. We all like the tetherball.

The third reason is that there are cracks in the basketball court. is dangerous! The hoops and nets are fine. Let's make our playground a safer place!

Talk with a partner about Jonathan's draft. Decide whether it has an opinion at the beginning. Can you find three good reasons for the opinion in this draft?

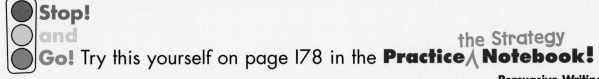

Revising

Add
(Elaborate)

Add facts to explain my reasons.

Now, it was time to **revise** my opinion speech. Every time I revise, I make my writing better! This time, I wanted to make sure I had all the facts I needed.

I decided to tell more about the swings and the basketball court. I used sticky notes to add facts to my opinion speech. Look on the next page. Find the facts I added.

Let's Fix Up Our Playground!

We should fix up our playground. One reason is that the swings are in bad shape. ∧The chains The swings look terrible.

The seats are torn.

The second reason we should fix up the playground is that the slide is old and wobbly. It shakes when you climb it. Nobody wants to use it. We all like the tetherball.

The third reason is that there are cracks in the basketball court. is dangerous! The hoops and nets are fine. Let's make our playground a safer place!

Sometimes people trip and fall.

Can you think of other ways to make Jonathan's draft better? Talk with a partner about your ideas.

Stop! and Go! Try this yourself on page 182 in the **Practice** the Strategy ∧ **Notebook!**

Revising

Take Out
(Clarify)

Take out sentences that don't help explain my opinion.

Next, I needed to see if there's anything in my opinion speech that shouldn't be there. I asked my writing partner, Ian, to listen as I read my speech.

Ian found two sentences that don't help explain why our playground needs to be fixed up. One is about the tetherball. The other is about the hoops and nets. I crossed out both of them.

Here's how my paper looks now.

[DRAFT]

Let's Fix Up Our Playground!
    We should fix up our playground.
One reason is that the swings are
in bad shape. ∧The chains The
swings look terrible.

> The seats are torn.

    The second reason we should fix
up the playground is that the slide
is old and wobbly. It shakes when
you climb it. Nobody wants to use
it. ~~We all like the tetherball.~~

    The third reason is that there
are cracks in the basketball court.
is dangerous! ↓~~The hoops and nets
are fine.~~ Let's make our playground
a safer place!

> Sometimes people trip and fall.

**Stop!
and
Go!** Try this yourself on page 183 in the **Practice** the Strategy ∧ **Notebook!**

Editing

Proofread

Make sure every sentence has a subject and a predicate.

Now it was time for fixing mistakes, or **editing**. As I proofread, I always check my spelling and grammar. I also needed to make sure that every sentence has a subject and a predicate. I had to add some subjects and predicates. I added periods where I added predicates to make complete sentences.

Subjects and Predicates

The **subject** of a sentence tells who or what does something.
The **predicate** tells what the subject does or is.
The predicate has the verb of the sentence.

Subject	Predicate
We	slide down fast.
The swings	need paint.
The park	is pretty.

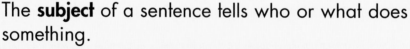

Extra Practice
See **Subjects and Predicates**
(pages CS 20–CS 2l) in the back of this book.

Here's how my speech looks after I edited it.

[DRAFT]

Let's Fix Up Our Playground!

We should fix up our playground. One reason is that the swings are in bad shape. ∧The chains ∧The swings look terrible.

are rusty.

The seats are torn.

The second reason we should fix up the playground is that the slide is old and wobbly. It shakes when you climb it. Nobody wants to use it. ~~We all like the tetherball.~~

The third reason is that there are cracks in the basketball court. is dangerous! ~~The hoops and nets are fine.~~ Let's make our playground a better, safer place!

Sometimes people trip and fall.

It

Publishing

Share

Give my speech during "Opinion Day" in my class.

You know that **publishing,** or sharing, is the last step in the writing process. This time, I shared my writing by giving the speech in my class. I also saved a copy of my speech. Here's what I did to publish my speech.

1. I copied my speech in my best handwriting and added my name. I included all the changes I made earlier.

2. My writing partner and I practiced reading our opinion speeches aloud to each other.

3. On Friday my class had "Opinion Day." We all read our opinion speeches to the class.

4. My teacher collected the opinion speeches and put them in a "Class Opinions Folder."

Class Opinion Day

Let's Fix Up Our Playground!
by Jonathan

We should fix up our playground. One reason is that the swings are in bad shape. The seats are torn. The chains are rusty. The swings look terrible.

The second reason we should fix up the playground is that the slide is old and wobbly. It shakes when you climb it. Nobody wants to use it.

The third reason is that there are cracks in the basketball court. It is dangerous! Sometimes people trip and fall. Let's make our playground a safer place!

USING the Rubric for Assessment

Go to page 186 in the **Practice** the Strategy **Notebook!** Use the rubric to check Jonathan's opinion speech.

Social Studies
Your Own Writing
PERSUASIVE

Use what you learned in this unit to write your own opinion paper, opinion speech, or both! Try these ideas.

- Use **Your Own Writing** pages in the *Practice the Strategy Notebook*.
- Pick a topic below, and write something new.
- Choose another idea of your own.

Follow the steps in the writing process. Use the Opinion Paper Rubric on pages 168–169 in the *Practice the Strategy Notebook* or the Opinion Speech Rubric on pages 186–187 in the *Practice the Strategy Notebook* to check your writing.

Opinion Paper

- what my community needs
- the best way to be a good citizen
- the most interesting part of my social studies book
- the best place to go in my town, city, or community

Opinion Speech

- where my class should go on a field trip to learn about history
- what should be added to my school to make it better
- what should be changed in my city, town, or neighborhood

portfolio

School–Home Connection

Keep a writing folder. Add **Your Own Writing** pages to your writing folder. You may want to take your writing folder home to share.

Writing to Take a Test

Test Writing
- ☑ starts with a writing prompt.
- ☑ may not let writers use outside sources.
- ☑ may have a time limit.
- ☑ may not allow writers to recopy.

Writing to Take a Test

Hi, I'm Danielle. Just like you, I have to take writing tests sometimes. Let me show you some tips. They will help you do well when you take a writing test.

Every writing test starts with a **writing prompt**. A writing prompt tells you what you are supposed to write. It also tells you what you should include to get a good grade. I'll show you how to read and understand a writing prompt. Once you know what to do, you can do great on any writing test!

Most writing prompts have three parts: the **Setup,** the **Task,** and the **Scoring Guide**. You need to read the writing prompt carefully. These three parts may not be labeled.

Can you find the three parts in this writing prompt?

Did you ever lose something? What did you do to try to get it back? Did you find it?

Write a story about what happened when you lost something.

Be sure your story
- tells the readers who was in the story and what happened.
- has a beginning, middle, and end.
- has details to make the story and the characters more interesting.
- doesn't have any sentences that don't belong.
- uses correct grammar, punctuation, and spelling.

Setup

Did you ever lose something? What did you do to try to get it back? Did you find it?

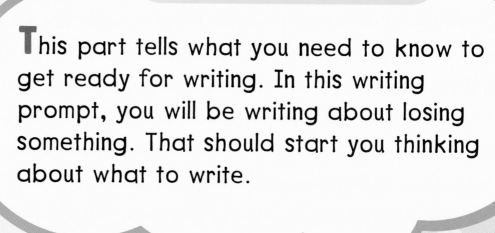

This part tells what you need to know to get ready for writing. In this writing prompt, you will be writing about losing something. That should start you thinking about what to write.

Task

Write a story about what happened when you lost something.

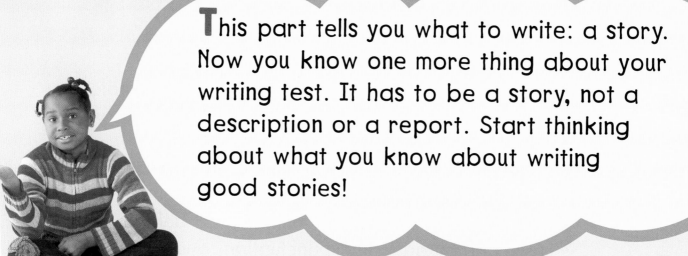

This part tells you what to write: a story. Now you know one more thing about your writing test. It has to be a story, not a description or a report. Start thinking about what you know about writing good stories!

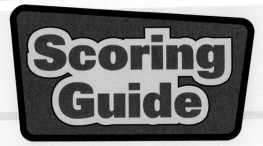

Scoring Guide

Be sure your story

- tells the readers who was in the story and what happened.
- has a beginning, middle, and end.
- has details to make the story and the characters more interesting.
- doesn't have any sentences that don't belong.
- uses correct grammar, punctuation, and spelling.

This is a very important part of the writing prompt. It tells how your writing will be scored. The Scoring Guide is a lot like a rubric. Each statement on the Scoring Guide tells you what to do, just like a rubric. If you follow the Scoring Guide and do what it says, you will do well on any writing test.

Using the Scoring Guide

to Study the Model

Let's see how my friend Allie did on her writing test. Here is the writing prompt again. Allie's test is on the next page.

Did you ever lose something? What did you do to try to get it back? Did you find it?

Write a story about what happened when you lost something.

Be sure your story
- tells the readers who was in the story and what happened.
- has a beginning, middle, and end.
- has details to make the story and the characters more interesting.
- doesn't have any sentences that don't belong.
- uses correct grammar, punctuation, and spelling.

Missing Cinders
by Allie James

A few months ago, Cinders disappeared. Cinders is my cute gray kitten. At first, I wasn't worried. Cinders loves to play outside. But this time was different. Cinders didn't come back when I called her.

This was the day my cousin Dora came to visit. She brought her dog with her. If there is one thing Cinders hates, it's dogs! She ran up a tree and wouldn't come down. Later that night, we were playing a game. I forgot that Cinders was outside.

The next day, Cinders still didn't come home. I started to worry. I asked if anyone had seen her. I put up signs around the neighborhood. Still, there was no sign of Cinders!

A week went by. I started to think Cinders would never come home again. I was really sad. My dad asked me if I wanted to get a new cat. But what I really wanted was for Cinders to come home.

One morning I went outside to get the newspaper for Dad. Just then I heard a tiny meow. Then Cinders crawled out from under a bush. I was so happy to see her! From now on, I'm going to start walking her on a leash!

Now we'll use the Scoring Guide to see how well Allie did. Remember, it's a lot like using a rubric. We'll read the statements from the Scoring Guide. Then, we'll see how well Allie did on each one.

Scoring Guide

The story tells the readers who was in the story and what happened.

Audience

In the first two sentences, Allie wrote that her kitten disappeared. That tells us right away who was in the story and what happened.

A few months ago, Cinders disappeared. Cinders is my cute gray kitten.

Scoring Guide

The story has a beginning, middle, and end.

Organization

Allie told about everything in the order it happened. She made it easy to follow the events. She used words like **Later that night** and **The next day** to show the order of events.

She ran up a tree and wouldn't come down. Later that night, we were playing a game. I forgot that Cinders was outside.

The next day, Cinders still didn't come home.

Scoring Guide

The story has details to make the story and the characters more interesting.

Elaboration

Allie included details to let readers know what her cat looks like and how she acts.

Cinders is my cute gray kitten. At first, I wasn't worried. Cinders loves to play outside.

Scoring Guide

The story doesn't have any sentences that don't belong.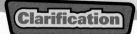

Clarification

Every sentence tells about Cinders being lost and getting found again. Here are some sentences about how much Allie missed Cinders.

I started to think Cinders would never come home again. I was really sad. My dad asked me if I wanted to get a new cat. But what I really wanted was for Cinders to come home.

Scoring Guide

The story uses correct grammar, punctuation, and spelling.

Conventions & Skills

Allie began each sentence with a capital letter and ended it with the correct punctuation mark. Every sentence has a subject and a predicate. Here is a sentence that shows strong feelings. It begins with a capital letter and ends with an exclamation point. Can you find the subject and the predicate?

I was so happy to see her!

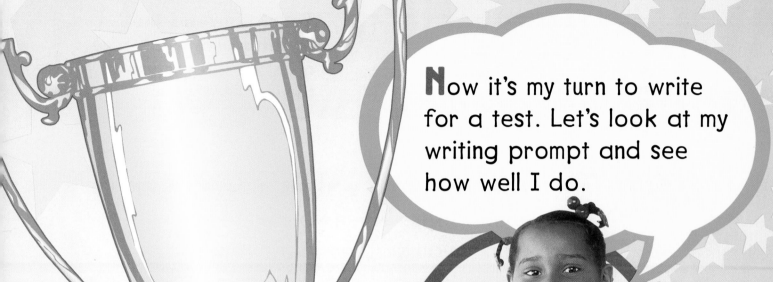

Now it's my turn to write for a test. Let's look at my writing prompt and see how well I do.

Danielle

Name: Danielle

Favorite Subject: science

Hobbies: working in my garden, playing basketball

Favorite Book: *Winnie-the-Pooh* by A.A. Milne

Assignment: writing a story for a test

Prewriting

Gather Ideas

Carefully read the writing prompt. Make a list of interesting topics. Pick one.

The first thing writers do is gather some ideas. When you write for a test, you gather ideas from the writing prompt. Here's my writing prompt.

Did you ever have a problem you needed to solve?

Write a story about what happened when you had a problem. Tell what happened first, next, and last. Tell how you solved the problem.

Be sure your story
- tells your readers who was in the story and what the problem was.
- tells the events in the order they happened.
- has details to make the story and the characters more interesting.
- doesn't have any sentences that don't belong.
- uses correct grammar, punctuation, and spelling.

I was supposed to write a story about a time when I had a problem. First, I did some **prewriting** to get ideas. I read the writing prompt again. I wrote down some topics and my thoughts about each topic. Then I picked a topic that fit the writing prompt.

My Topics

A boy in space makes a new friend.

How I studied for a test

I didn't know what to give my mom for her birthday.

My Thinking

This isn't about how I solved a problem. It doesn't fit the writing prompt.

This won't be very interesting for my readers.

This really fits the writing prompt. It's also an interesting topic for a story. I'll use this one!

Stop!
and
Go! Try this yourself on page 188 in the **Practice** the Strategy **Notebook!**

Prewriting

Organize

Plan my time.

When you take a writing test, you need to plan your time. First, be sure to spend some time planning what you will write. Give yourself lots of time to write your draft. Leave some time to read your draft and fix any mistakes.

Look at the clock on the next page. It shows how I planned my time for a writing test. If the test takes an hour, here's how I will use my time.

Prewriting
Organize   **Plan my time.**

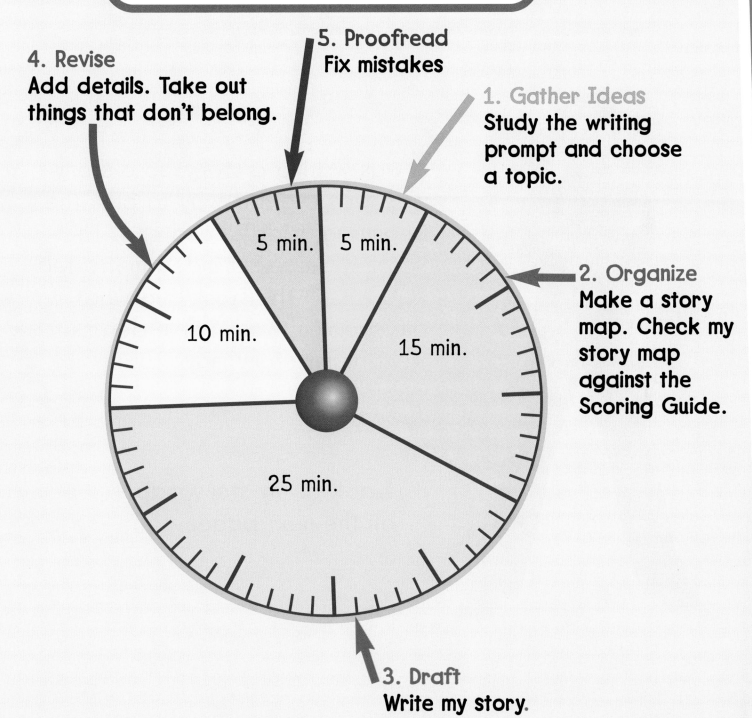

4. Revise
Add details. Take out things that don't belong.

5. Proofread
Fix mistakes

1. Gather Ideas
Study the writing prompt and choose a topic.

2. Organize
Make a story map. Check my story map against the Scoring Guide.

5 min.

5 min.

10 min.

15 min.

25 min.

3. Draft
Write my story.

Prewriting
Organize

Make a story map to tell who was in the story, what the problem was, and what happened.

I was writing a story, so a story map was a good way to plan the beginning, middle, and end. The Scoring Guide reminded me to tell who was in the story and what the problem was. These details went on my story map, too.

Look at my story map on the next page.

My Story: Mom's Best Birthday

Characters: my teacher, my neighbors, my mom, and me

Problem: I didn't know what to get my mom for her birthday.

What happened

Beginning

When I told my teacher my problem, she gave me some colored pencils and some cool paper.

Middle

Mrs. Lopez gave me a beautiful rose from her garden. Mr. Weng gave me a pretty ribbon.

End

I surprised my mom and made her happy.

Stop! and Go! Try this yourself on page 194 in the **Practice** the Strategy **Notebook!**

Prewriting
Organize
Check my story map against the Scoring Guide.

It's really important to prewrite on a test. That's because you don't get much time to revise. Before I wrote, I checked my story map against the Scoring Guide in the writing prompt.

Scoring Guide

Be sure your story tells your readers who is in the story.

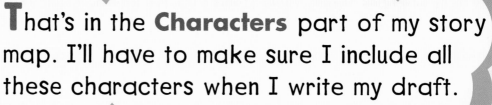

That's in the **Characters** part of my story map. I'll have to make sure I include all these characters when I write my draft.

Characters: my teacher, my neighbors, my mom, and me

Be sure your story tells what the problem was.

That's in the **Problem** part of my story map. I'll tell the problem at the beginning of my draft, so my readers will be interested in reading my story.

Problem: I didn't know what to get my mom for her birthday.

Be sure your story tells the events in the order they happened.

That's in the **What happened** part of my story map. I'll need to add some events and make sure they're in the right order when I write my story.

What happened

Beginning

When I told my teacher my problem, she gave me some colored pencils and some cool paper.

Middle

Mrs. Lopez gave me a beautiful rose from her garden. Mr. Weng gave me a pretty ribbon.

End

I surprised my mom and made her happy.

Scoring Guide

Be sure your story has details to make the story and the characters more interesting.

I'll add some details as I write my draft. I want my story and my characters to be interesting.

Scoring Guide

Be sure your story doesn't have any sentences that don't belong.

I'll read my story later to make sure all of the sentences are about the problem I had and how I solved it.

Scoring Guide

Be sure your story uses correct grammar, punctuation, and spelling.

I'll check that part later, too. I want to make sure that every sentence is right.

Drafting
Write

Use my story map. Write sentences to tell what happened at the beginning, middle, and end, and how the problem was solved.

Next, I used my story map to **draft**, or write, my story. I knew that I would go back and fix mistakes later, so I didn't worry about them too much for now.

I skipped lines as I wrote my story. That way, I would have room to add things and fix any mistakes. I tried to write as neatly as I could because I knew I wouldn't be able to recopy my story later. Read my draft on the next page.

I had a problem and I didnt know what to do. It was a few days before my mom's birthday. I didn't know what to get for her. My teacher asked what was wrong. I told her. She said she was sure I would think of something. Then she gave me some colored pencils and some cool paper.

I still didn't have any ideas. My neighbor, Mrs. lopez, saw me looking sad. It was the day before Mom's birthday. She gave me a beautiful rose from her garden. Then she said she was sure I would think of something.

the morning of my mom's birthday. Mr. weng waved as I walked by his store He gave me a pretty gold ribbon. then he told me not to worry about my mom's birthday. I still didnt have a gift for her.

That afternoon, I had an idea. I called my best friend. I watched some TV. I made a birthday card with my new cool paper and colored pencils. It said "Happy Birthday, Mom!" Then I tied the pretty ribbon around the rose. When Mom came in, I gave her the card and the rose. said the rose and the card were pretty. Her favorite sport is bowling. Mom said it was the best present ever because I made it myself. said it was the best birthday she ever had.

Stop! and Go! Try this yourself on page 198 in the **Practice** the Strategy **Notebook!**

Revising

Add (Elaborate)

Add details to make the story and characters more interesting.

On a test, I can't talk with my writing partner, so I always reread my story to myself. The Scoring Guide says to include details that make the story and the characters interesting. I decided to add more details about the pencils and paper and how my teacher knew I had a problem. I also added a detail about Mr. Weng.

I can't use sticky notes on a writing test, so I used proofreading marks to add my details. I'm glad I skipped lines when I wrote my draft!

I had a problem and I didnt know what to do. It was a few days before my mom's birthday. I didn't know what to get for her, My teacher asked what was wrong. I told her.
^I must have looked kind of sad.

She said she was sure I would think of something. Then she gave me some colored pencils and some cool paper.
^green and blue ^with silver and gold designs

I still didn't have any ideas. My neighbor, Mrs. lopez, saw me looking sad. It was the day before Mom's birthday. She gave me a beautiful rose from her garden. Then she said she was sure I would think of something.

the morning of my mom's birthday. Mr. weng waved as I walked by his store He gave me a pretty gold ribbon. then he told me not to worry about my mom's birthday. I still didnt have a gift for her.
^Mr. Weng is a decorator.

That afternoon, I had an idea. I called my best friend. I watched some TV. I made a birthday card with my new cool paper and colored pencils. It said "Happy Birthday, Mom!" Then I tied the pretty ribbon around the rose. When Mom came in, I gave her the card and the rose. said the rose and the card were pretty. Her favorite sport is bowling. Mom said it was the best present ever because I made it myself. said it was the best birthday she ever had.

Stop!
and
Go! Try this yourself on page 202 in the **Practice**˄ **Notebook!**
the Strategy

Revising

Take Out
(Clarify)

Take out sentences that don't help tell what happened.

I read the Scoring Guide again to make sure I was doing everything it says. The Scoring Guide says that I need to make sure my story doesn't have any sentences that don't belong. I read my story again and found three sentences that don't help tell what happened in my story. I crossed them out.

I had a problem and I didnt know what to do. It was a
few days before my mom's birthday. I didn't know what to

I must have looked kind of sad.
get for her. My teacher asked what was wrong. I told her.
                 ^
She said she was sure I would think of something. Then she
                  green and blue   with silver and gold designs
gave me some colored pencils and some cool paper.
              ^   ^

I still didn't have any ideas. My neighbor, Mrs. lopez,

saw me looking sad. It was the day before Mom's birthday.

She gave me a beautiful rose from her garden. Then she

said she was sure I would think of something.

the morning of my mom's birthday. Mr. weng waved as
                    Mr. Weng is a decorator.
I walked by his store. He gave me a pretty gold ribbon.
                       ^
then he told me not to worry about my mom's birthday. I

still didnt have a gift for her.

That afternoon, I had an idea. ~~I called my best friend. I~~

~~watched some TV.~~ I made a birthday card with my new

cool paper and colored pencils. It said "Happy Birthday,

Mom!" Then I tied the pretty ribbon around the rose. When

Mom came in, I gave her the card and the rose. said the

rose and the card were pretty. ~~Her favorite sport is~~

~~bowling.~~ Mom said it was the best present ever because I

made it myself. said it was the best birthday she ever had.

Editing

Proofread

Make sure every sentence begins with a capital letter and ends with correct punctuation and has a subject and a predicate.

I always check my paper one last time for mistakes. The Scoring Guide says that my story needs to have correct grammar, punctuation, and spelling. First, I wanted to make sure my sentences begin and end correctly and are complete.

I also wanted to make sure that I used good grammar, punctuation, and spelling in my story. Using a checklist of rules is a big help. We've talked about these rules so often that I almost know them by heart. Read the checklist on the next page.

Proofreading Checklist

☑ Does each sentence begin with a capital letter and end with the right punctuation mark?

☑ Are all contractions written correctly?

☑ Are all regular plural nouns written correctly?

☑ Does every proper noun begin with a capital letter?

☑ Are all quotation marks used correctly?

☑ Does every sentence have a subject and a predicate?

Extra Practice
See **Review**
(pages CS 22–CS 23) in the back of this book.

I kept the checklist in mind as I edited my story. Look on the next page to see how I did.

I corrected all the mistakes I found. I also added a title and my name to my story. I can't recopy my paper because this is a test. That's OK, though. I can turn it in with all the corrections. This is how my story looked after I edited it.

Proofreading Marks

≡ Make a capital letter.

/ Make a small letter.

∧ Add something.

— Take out something.

⊙ Add a period.

¶ New paragraph

Mom's Best Birthday

by Danielle

I had a problem and I didn't know what to do. It was a few days before my mom's birthday. I didn't know what to

I must have looked kind of sad.

get for her. My teacher asked what was wrong. I told her.

She said she was sure I would think of something. Then she

green and blue   with silver and gold designs

gave me some colored pencils and some cool paper.

I still didn't have any ideas. My neighbor, Mrs. lopez, saw me looking sad. It was the day before Mom's birthday. She gave me a beautiful rose from her garden. Then she said she was sure I would think of something.

It was ∧ the morning of my mom's birthday. Mr. weng waved as
Mr. Weng is a decorator.
I walked by his store ⊙ He gave me a pretty gold ribbon.
then he told me not to worry about my mom's birthday. I
still didn∧t have a gift for her.

That afternoon, I had an idea. ~~I called my best friend. I watched some TV.~~ I made a birthday card with my new cool paper and colored pencils. It said "Happy Birthday, Mom!" Then I tied the pretty ribbon around the rose. When
Mom came in, I gave her the card and the rose ∧ said the
                                              She
rose and the card were pretty. ~~Her favorite sport is bowling.~~ Mom said it was the best present ever because I
made it myself ∧ said it was the best birthday she ever had.
              She

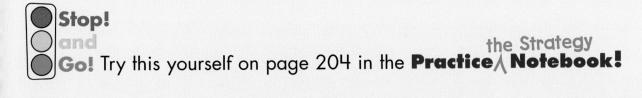

test tips

I'm done! Writing for a test is a little different from other writing. Remember these tips when you write for a test.

1. **Carefully read the writing prompt before you start to write.**
   Remember, most writing prompts have three parts: the **Setup**, the **Task**, and the **Scoring Guide**.

2. **Make sure you know what to do before you write. Remember to**
   - read the prompt carefully.
   - understand what you need to do.
   - make sure you know how your writing will be graded.

3. **Plan your time.**
Think about how much time to use for each step:
- Gathering Ideas
- Organizing
- Drafting
- Revising
- Proofreading

4. **Reread your writing. Check it against the Scoring Guide.**
A Scoring Guide on a writing test is a lot like a rubric. It can help you remember what's important, so you can get a good grade.

5. **Plan, plan, plan!**
You don't get much time to revise during a test. Plan ahead!

6. **Write neatly.**
Remember, it doesn't matter how good your story is if your readers can't read your writing!

Stop!
and
Go! to page 206 in the **Practice** the Strategy **Notebook!**

Your Own Writing TEST

Try out the tips you practiced in this unit. Choose one of the ideas below or come up with your own idea. Then take your own writing "test." Pretend this is a real test. Give yourself one hour to finish all of the steps. Use one of these ideas.

Write a story about a problem you had and how you solved it.

OR

Write a story about a time you had a lot of fun.

OR

Write a story about the first time you tried something new.

Be sure your story

- tells the readers who was in the story and what happened.
- has a beginning, middle, and end.
- has details to make the story and the characters more interesting.
- doesn't have sentences that don't belong.
- uses correct grammar, punctuation, and spelling.

portfolio

School–Home Connection

Keep a writing folder. Add **Your Own Writing** pages to your writing folder. You may want to take your writing folder home to share.

Extra Practice

conventions & Skills

Do you need some more practice with the editing skills you worked on in this book? Use the activities in this section to get more practice. Complete each activity on a separate sheet of paper.

Table of Contents

Capitalizing and Punctuating Sentences

A **sentence** is a group of words that tells a complete thought.

Review the Rule

Begin each sentence with a capital letter. End each sentence with a period (unless the sentence asks a question or shows strong feelings).

Practice

Number your paper 1.–20. Read each sentence. Rewrite the incorrect sentences. Put in any missing capital letters and periods. If a sentence is correct, write **Correct** after the number.

   1. We go to the pool

   2. our mom watches us.

   3. My brother jumps into the pool

   4. the water is cold

   5. I get in slowly.

   6. I put just my feet in first

   7. then I get my legs wet.

8. next, I get my arms and body wet

9. My head is the last part to go into the water.

10. now I am all wet.

11. my brother splashes me.

12. I want to splash him back.

13. He swims away from me

14. I don't swim after him

15. soon I will learn to swim

16. I don't know how to yet

17. then I will chase my brother

18. I will swim fast.

19. we will have lots of fun in the pool

20. the pool is a great place.

Apply

Copy this paragraph on your paper. Add capital letters and periods where they are needed.

Meg learned to swim. First, she learned to put her face in the water Next, she learned to float. then she learned to kick. Finally, she learned how to use her arms. now, Meg can swim across the pool

Parts of a Friendly Letter

A **friendly letter** is written to someone you know. You can tell a story in the letter. A friendly letter has five parts.

Review the Rule

- The **heading** gives your address and the date. It has three lines.
  The first line is your street address.
  The next line is your city, state, and zip code.
  The last line is the date.

- The **greeting** begins with *Dear*. It ends with the name of the person you are writing to and a comma.

- The **body** is the main part of the letter. It is made up of sentences. It can tell a story.

- The **closing** is a word or two words like *Love, Your pal,* or *Your cousin*. The closing begins with a capital letter and ends with a comma.

- The **signature** is your name, written by you.

Practice

Number your paper 1.–5. Read the letter below.
Write the name of each numbered part.

1. 12 Elm Street
Durbin, ND 54321
May 21, 20- -

2. Dear Keith,

3. Yesterday, we got a new house! First, we looked
at a lot of homes. Then my parents talked it over.
Finally, they bought one on Shady Lane. It's great!
I'll give you my new address soon.

4. Your buddy,
5. Joe

Apply

This friendly letter is all mixed up. Rewrite it
correctly. You can use Joe's letter above to help you.

August 6, 20–
Your friend, Chris

We got a cat yesterday. First, we went to an animal
shelter. We saw lots of cats there. Then we picked out
Franny. Last, we took her home.

Dear George,
Miami, FL 43210
123 Palm Ave.

Sentences must begin with a **capital letter**. A sentence can **tell something**. A sentence can **ask a question**. A sentence can **show strong feelings**.

Review the Rule

- Begin every sentence with a capital letter.
- Put a period **(.)** after telling sentences.
- Put a question mark **(?)** after asking sentences.
- Put an exclamation point **(!)** after sentences that show strong feelings.

Practice

Number your paper 1.–20. Read each sentence. Rewrite incorrect sentences so they start with capital letters and end with the correct punctuation. If a sentence has no errors, write **Correct**.

1. My dad takes me to the store
2. What should we buy to eat
3. I love to shop
4. we buy food for the week.
5. dad likes lots of fruit.

6. He buys things for salad.

7. I pick out two kinds of yogurt.

8. mom wants fish and meat

9. Do you think the fruit smells good

10. buying cereal is my job.

11. Which cereal should we buy this week

12. I buy Puff Pops.

13. Next, we pick out bread

14. Dad gets two cartons of milk.

15. I ask for some juice.

16. the basket is so heavy!

17. How long will it take to check out

18. we leave the store

19. We fill up the car with bags.

20. I am glad to go home

Apply

Read the paragraph below. Write the paragraph correctly on a separate piece of paper by adding capital letters and correct punctuation.

We go to Scali Bakery. What makes it smell so good inside There are all kinds of breads. there are rows of cookies, too. Near the window are many kinds of cakes. some of them are for birthday parties. All of them look so good

Contractions

A **contraction** is made up of two words put together. Some letters from the two words are left out. An apostrophe (') takes the place of the missing letters.

Review the Rule

Two words	Take out	Add apostrophe	Contraction
can + not	the **no** in **not**	'	can't
did + not	the **o** in **not**	'	didn't
do + not	the **o** in **not**	'	don't
does + not	the **o** in **not**	'	doesn't
it + is	the **i** in **is**	'	it's
they + are	the **a** in **are**	'	they're

Practice

Number your paper 1.–20. Read each sentence. Write the words in parentheses as a contraction.

1. (I will) show you my pet.
2. (It is) a goldfish.
3. (Is not) she pretty?
4. She (cannot) talk.
5. She (does not) run.

6. She (has not) ever laughed.

7. (She is) a great pet, though.

8. (Do not) you want one?

9. (You will) get one, too.

10. (You are) going to love it.

11. (I have) got two pet frogs.

12. (He is) Danny.

13. (She is) Frannie.

14. (They are) cute.

15. Danny (does not) jump a lot.

16. (He is) not happy.

17. My mom (did not) want me to get them.

18. Mom says frogs (are not) good pets.

19. A frog (should not) be in a little bowl.

20. (It is) happier in a big pond.

Apply

Correct any contractions that are not written correctly. Write the paragraph with the correct contractions on a separate piece of paper.

My fish tank doe'snt have any goldfish. Its' full of sharks instead! Theyre small silver sharks that cant hurt you. At first, I did'nt want to get them. Now I dont' want any other kind of fish!

Plural Nouns

A **plural noun** names more than one person, place, or thing. In most cases, add *-s* to a noun to make it plural. Add *-es* to nouns that end in *x*, *ch*, *s*, or *sh*. Don't use an apostrophe (') to make a noun plural.

Review the Rule

One		Plural Noun	One		Plural Noun
student	+ s	students	fox	+ es	foxes
town	+ s	towns	bench	+ es	benches
tree	+ s	trees	crash	+ es	crashes

Practice

Number your paper 1.–20. Write the plural of each noun.

1. storm
2. sand
3. dress
4. home
5. girl

6. brush
7. root
8. hall
9. box
10. couch

11. boy
12. trip
13. planet
14. star
15. stone
16. apple
17. pen
18. car
19. team
20. truck

21. letter
22. pencil
23. dish
24. ax
25. top
26. wrench
27. flower
28. tree
29. flash
30. paper

Apply

Read the paragraph below. Look for errors in plural nouns. Write the paragraph correctly on a separate piece of paper.

We look at the weather map. Weather map's show frontses. A front is the place where cold air meets warm air. Weather reporterss use frontses to predict the weather. Sometimes, reportes for the same area are different. That is because many different thingses change the weather.

A sentence can make a statement, ask a question, give a command, or express strong feelings. It begins with a **capital letter** and ends with a **punctuation mark**.

Review the Rule

Begin every sentence with a capital letter. Use a period to end a statement. Use a question mark to end a question. Use an exclamation point to end a sentence that shows strong feelings.

Practice

Number your paper 1.–20. Read each sentence. If the sentence is punctuated correctly, write **Correct**. If the sentence has a mistake in punctuation, write the sentence correctly on your paper.

1. How many continents does Earth have.

2. Did you know Earth has seven continents.

3. I can name all seven of them.

4. They are Africa, Antarctica, Asia, Australia, Europe, North America, and South America.

5. That's amazing?

6. Do many people live in Asia.

7. Most of the people on Earth live in Asia.

8. How interesting that is!

9. Is Australia a continent or an island!

10. What a question you ask?

11. Australia is both a continent and an island.

12. If you live in the United States, you live in North America?

13. On what continent would you find Egypt?

14. Egypt is in Africa.

15. What is the coldest continent!

16. Antarctica has the coldest weather of all?

17. Did you know that most of that continent is covered in ice.

18. Boy, am I glad we don't live there!

19. Europe has many people in it.

20. Can you find it on a map?

Apply

Read the paragraph below. Look for mistakes in punctuation. Write the paragraph correctly on a separate piece of paper.

Our class is learning about continents? Did you know that continents move. That's amazing. Sometimes they crash into each other. Is that how mountains form. Many mountains were formed that way.

Proper Nouns

A **proper noun** is the name of a person, place, or thing.
A proper noun begins with a capital letter.

Review the Rule

Begin a person's first and last names with a capital letter.

    Bill **G**reen   **S**ally **C**hang   **C**hris **J**ohnson

Begin place names with capital letters.

    France   **L**incoln **S**chool   **E**lm **R**oad

Begin the names of specific things, like days, months, and holidays, with a capital letter.

    Monday   **J**anuary   **L**abor **D**ay

Practice

Number your paper 1.–20. If a proper noun in the sentence does not begin with a capital letter, write the proper noun correctly. If the proper noun already begins with a capital letter, write **Correct**.

  1. We went to the Smith Library.

  2. It is on market street.

  3. We went there on friday.

  4. It was the first day of march.

  5. Mrs. cole showed us where to find fairy tales.

6. Matt likes books about hansel and gretel.

7. Nicki likes books about peter pan.

8. I showed a book about four hens to tom.

9. He showed me a book of stories from Mexico.

10. May took out a book of stories from china.

11. Mr. blake is the librarian.

12. He read us stories told by Neil Philip.

13. The stories came from a place called arabia.

14. One of them was about a man named ali baba.

15. He had a brother named kasim.

16. Ali Baba was poor, and his brother was rich.

17. One day, ali baba met forty thieves.

18. I liked the story, and so did bobby.

19. Later, amy checked the book out of the library.

20. I will check it out in april.

Apply

Read this paragraph. Find all proper nouns that are not written correctly. Write the paragraph correctly on a separate piece of paper.

My friend, paul, told me a story that comes from africa. It is about a spider. The spider's name is anansi. He loves to trick everybody! The stories are funny. Sometimes the spider gets into trouble. You can find the stories at the wilson library. It is open every day but sunday.

Quotation marks (" ") show where the words someone says begin and end.

Review the Rule

Use quotation marks to show where a speaker begins talking and where he or she stops talking.

- Ms. Neal said, "I will read you a story."
- "What is it about?" asked Bob.

Practice

Number your paper 1.–20. Rewrite all incorrect sentences by adding the missing quotation marks. If a sentence is correct, write **Correct** after the number.

1. Ms. Neal said, This story is about a dog and a bone.

2. She said, "It is a good story.

3. She began, "A dog was carrying a bone."

4. Then she said, "It looked into a lake."

5. What did the dog see?" asked Katie.

6. "It saw a dog in the water carrying a bone!" Ms. Neal answered.

7. The dog said, That dog has a bone, too!

8. It looks better than my bone," the dog added.

9. Nolan asked, What happened?"

10. Ms. Neal laughed.

11. She said, "The dog dropped the bone!

12. Jenna asked, "Why?"

13. He wanted the other bone," said Ms. Neal.

14. Ms. Neal added, "But now the dog had no bone at all!"

15. "Is that a fable? asked Terry.

16. Yes, answered Ms. Neal.

17. I know the lesson! shouted Rico.

18. "What is it? asked Ms. Neal.

19. Rico said, "Don't want what someone else has."

20. That's great! said Ms. Neal.

Apply

Add quotation marks wherever they are needed and rewrite this fable on your paper.

A boy saw candy in a jar. He asked his mother, May I have some?

She said, You may have a little.

The boy put his hand in and grabbed lots of candy. Then he couldn't get his hand out.

My hand is stuck! he cried.

The lesson is that a little at a time is better than none at all.

Subjects and Predicates

The **subject** of a sentence tells who or what does or is something. The **predicate** of a sentence tells what the subject does or is.

Review the Rule

Every sentence needs both a subject and a predicate.

Subject	Predicate
My favorite food	is noodles.
The bread	bakes in the oven.

Practice

Number your paper **1.–20.** Write **S** if the underlined words are the subject. Write **P** if the underlined words are the predicate.

1. My friend Jen eats with us.
2. My dad makes hamburgers.
3. We eat potatoes, too.
4. A big salad is part of the meal.
5. I drink milk with my meal.
6. Jen has a glass of water.

7. One big hamburger is enough for me!

8. Jen's family invites me to dinner.

9. Her mother makes pasta.

10. The noodles taste great.

11. Red sauce covers them.

12. I dip a big piece of bread in the sauce.

13. The tomato sauce is hot.

14. It tastes a little spicy.

15. A big plate of spaghetti is just right for me.

16. That much spaghetti is too much for Jen.

17. Jen's mom offers us dessert.

18. We are both too full.

19. I say thank you.

20. My stomach feels full and happy.

Apply

Find any sentences in this paragraph that are missing a subject or a predicate. Write the paragraph correctly on a separate piece of paper. You will have to add some words.

My favorite snack is cheese and crackers. taste great together. Whole wheat crackers. Sometimes I have a big glass of milk, too. fills me up fast. I like to have my snack when I get home from school.

The **subject** of a sentence tells who or what does or is something. The **predicate** of a sentence tells what the subject does or is.

Review the Rule

Every sentence needs both a subject and a predicate.

Subject	Predicate
The children	like the swings.
They	are new and shiny.

Practice

Number your paper 1.–20. Write **Subject** if the underlined words are the subject. Write **Predicate** if the underlined words are the predicate.

1. Big Tree Park <u>is on Pine Street</u>.
2. <u>The park</u> has a new playground.
3. <u>My friends</u> like the slide there.
4. They <u>go down it all day long</u>!
5. The park <u>has great swings, too</u>.
6. <u>They</u> are brand new.

7. <u>Maria</u> swings high on them.

8. Rob <u>loves the tire swings</u>.

9. The hopscotch board <u>is always busy</u>.

10. The <u>pond</u> is nearby.

11. <u>People</u> can't swim there.

12. <u>Ducks</u> like it, though.

13. We <u>run up and down on poles and bars</u>.

14. Rope bridges <u>shake under us</u>.

15. Rope ladders <u>hold our weight</u>.

16. <u>My friend Mike</u> spent all day there.

17. <u>We</u> play for hours.

18. <u>My dad</u> takes us to the park often.

19. Mike's older sister <u>drives us there once a week</u>.

20. <u>I</u> feel happy at that park!

Apply

Read this paragraph. Find any sentences that are missing a subject or a predicate. Write the paragraph correctly on a separate piece of paper.

Some parents wanted a new playground for us. Held a meeting. Asked us for ideas. One weekend we all built it together. Many parents, children, and other volunteers. It was fun to do. Now we have a great playground.

Proofreading Checklist

☑ Does each sentence begin with a capital letter and end with the right punctuation mark?

☑ Are all contractions written correctly?

☑ Are all regular plural nouns written correctly?

☑ Does every proper noun begin with a capital letter?

☑ Are all quotation marks used correctly?

☑ Does every sentence have a subject and a predicate?

Practice

Number your paper 1.–20. Rewrite each incorrect sentence to correct errors in grammar, capitalization, or punctuation. Add any missing subjects or predicates. If a sentence has no errors, write **Correct**.

1. I love birthday parties

2. morgan brought pretty balloons.

3. played games.

4. all my friends were there.

5. My pet kitten, henry.

6. Sam blew out the candles

7. We ate chocolate cake.

8. he wished for some book's.

9. Everyone brought a present.

10. opened a present.

11. Sam jumped up and down.

12. the present was a book.

13. We clapped our hands

14. the book was about animals.

15. It had many pictures.

16. had a red ribbon.

17. Sam opened the next present.

18. the box had another book inside.

19. Everyone laughed

20. was the same book.

Apply

Copy this thank-you note on your paper. Add any missing subjects or predicates. Correct any errors in grammar, capital letters, or punctuation.

Dear sam,

the party was great I thank you for asking me. I had a fun time The chocolate cake. I hope you like the book. My teacher helped me pick it out. knows about bookss.

Your friend,

max

Publishing

Editing

Prewriting

Gather Ideas

Organize

Add

Take Out

Revising

Drafting

Writer's Handbook

Table of Contents

Prewriting
Gather Ideas

Brainstorming

Brainstorming is saying things as you think of them. You can do this alone or with a writing partner. You can also do this in a small group. Let's say you are going to write a report about an animal. How do you pick an animal? Maybe you have a pet. Maybe you read a book about animals. Maybe you went to the zoo. Start naming some animals. Take turns if you are working with others. Write down the animals you say. One of them might become a good topic for your report.

Daydreaming/Doodling

Daydreaming is letting your mind wander. Pick a quiet place. Then ask yourself a question that gets you wondering. Here are some good questions to ask.

- "What will I be when I grow up?"

- "What would it be like to live under the sea?"

- "Is there life in outer space?"

Let your imagination take over. You might be surprised at the good ideas that come to you.

Doodling is another word for drawing. Start with a pencil and some clean paper. Draw anything you think of. Look at your doodles. One of them could be a great idea for your next writing project.

Interviewing

An interview is a conversation. Talk to people who know about your topic. You can talk to family members or to other people. If you want to write about baking a cake, talk to someone who bakes. It could be someone in your family or it could be a baker in your town. Ask questions. Listen to people's answers and stories and jot down some notes. It's a good idea to take your parents with you when you talk to other adults.

Favorite Books, Movies, and TV Shows

- What books do you like?
- What movies and shows do you watch?

Do you like books about make-believe animals?
  Try writing a story about a dragon.

Do you like movies about space?
  Try writing about a space trip.

Do you like TV shows about kids?
  Try writing a story about you and your friends.

My Topic: Lizards
What I know:
- have scales
- animals
- green

Lists

Lists are good tools for all kinds of things. We make lists to shop. We make lists for chores. We make lists to remember things. Writers make lists, too. A list can tell you what you already know about your topic. A list can help you figure out what you need to know. Write a list of things you already know about your topic. Then write a list of things you don't know. Find out the things you need to know. Put them together with what you already know. Now you have everything you need for writing.

What I don't know:
- what they eat
- where they live
- what kinds there are

Notes

Notes are good tools for jotting down information. You can take notes from books or articles. You can take notes from interviews. Write down the important parts. Keep your notes short. Write clearly because you will need to read your notes later. You can use paper or note cards. Leave two lines between your notes on paper. This makes the notes easier to read. It also leaves room for more notes. Use one note card for each note. You can even use note cards in different colors. Keep your notes in one place. That way you can find them when you need to use them for your writing.

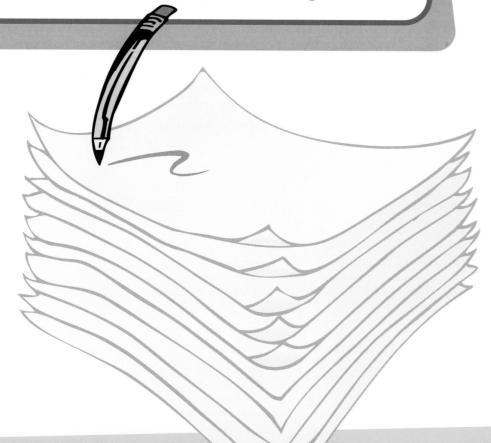

Prewriting Organize

Storyboard

Use a storyboard to plan a story. A storyboard shows the events of a story in order. This storyboard shows the events of a story about a boy's first swimming lesson.

Topic: My First Swimming Lesson

1 Me

2

3

Five Senses Chart

Use a five senses chart to plan a description or a report. A five senses chart tells how something looks, sounds, tastes, feels, and smells. This five senses chart organizes information for a descriptive paper about a neighborhood market.

Subject of My Paper: The Super T	
I can see	• mangoes and kiwis • herbs • strings of chili peppers • spices
I can hear	• people talking • cash register • music playing beeping
I can taste	I can't taste anything at the Super T unless I buy it.
I can touch (feel)	• mangoes and kiwis • chili peppers
I can smell	• mangoes and kiwis • herbs • chili peppers • spices

Venn Diagram

Use a Venn diagram to plan a description of two things or a compare-and-contrast paper. A Venn diagram shows how two things are the same and different. This Venn diagram organizes information for a compare-and-contrast paper about goldfish and frogs.

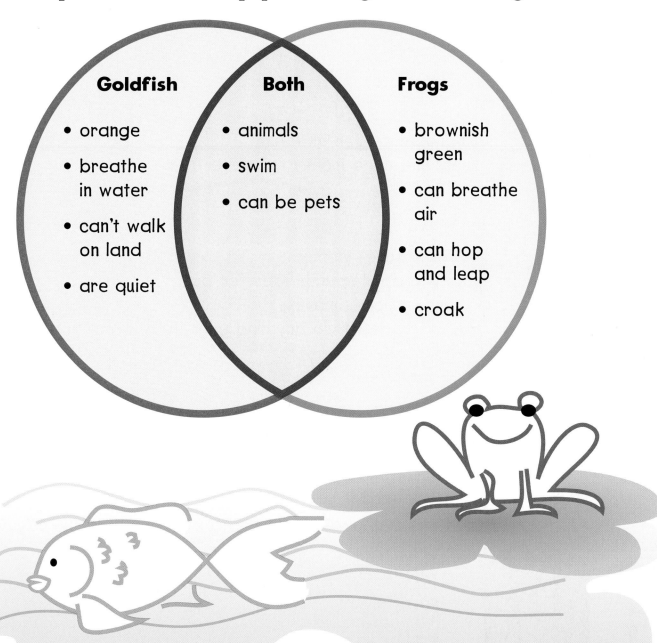

Goldfish

- orange
- breathe in water
- can't walk on land
- are quiet

Both

- animals
- swim
- can be pets

Frogs

- brownish green
- can breathe air
- can hop and leap
- croak

Story Map

Use a story map to plan a story. A story map tells who is in the story. It tells what the problem is. Finally, it tells what happens in the story and how the problem is solved. This story map shows the beginning, middle, and end of a fable about two sisters.

Beginning

Characters—Jen and Jule
Problem—need money for water park

Middle

Jen— saves money,
          does special jobs for pay
Jule—spends money,
          doesn't do anything extra

End

Jen—   has money to go
Jule—   has no money to go
Lesson—Plan ahead and work
          hard if you want something.

Order Chain

Use an order chain to plan a how-to paper or a report. An order chain tells steps in order. This order chain shows the steps of making a jigsaw puzzle for a how-to paper.

Topic: How to Make a Jigsaw Puzzle

First Step Find a picture in a magazine and cut it out.

Next Step Cut a piece of heavy paper the same size as the picture.

Next Step Paste the picture on the heavy paper.

Next Step Wait for the paste to dry. Draw two wavy lines across and two wavy lines down the back of the paper.

Last Step Cut the picture apart on the lines.

Web

Use a web to plan a report, a description, or a story. A web has the topic in the center. It has details around the topic. Sometimes the center of the web has a question. This web helps organize information for a report on clouds. It answers the question, "What are clouds?"

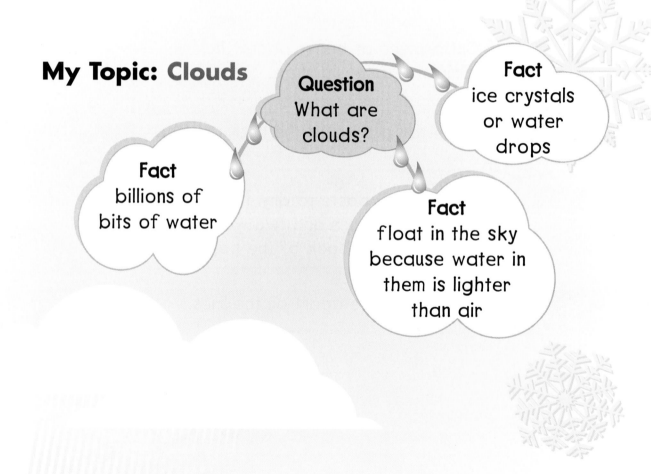

My Topic: Clouds

Question What are clouds?

Fact ice crystals or water drops

Fact billions of bits of water

Fact float in the sky because water in them is lighter than air

Spider Map

Use a spider map to plan a report or a description.
A spider map has the topic in the spider's "body."
It has details on the spider's "legs." This spider map
shows why lasagna makes the best meal for a
persuasive paper about favorite foods.

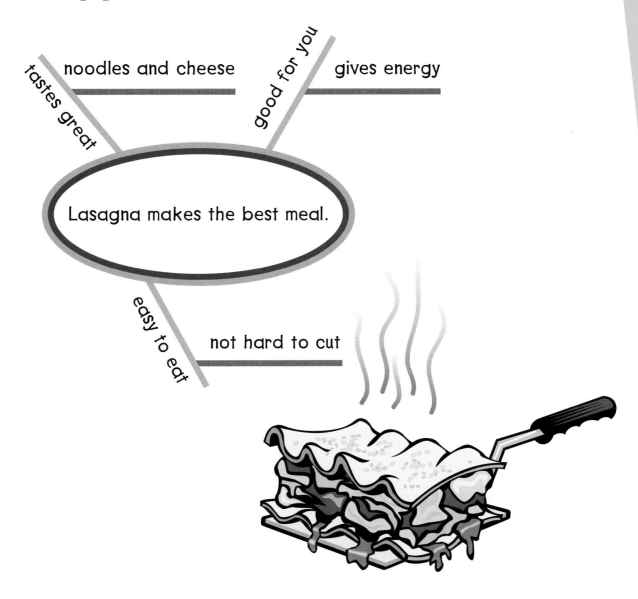

noodles and cheese

good for you

gives energy

tastes great

Lasagna makes the best meal.

easy to eat

not hard to cut

Writing Sentences

A sentence is a group of words that tells a complete idea. Sentences have a subject. The subject is the person or thing doing something. Sentences have a predicate. The predicate is what the subject is doing. Read these two groups of words. Which one is not a sentence?

Becca ran home.

Raining hard.

The first group of words is a sentence. How can you tell? It has a subject, someone who is doing something—*Becca*. What did Becca do? She ran home. That's the predicate—*ran home*. This is a complete sentence.

The second group of words is not a sentence. Does it have a subject, or a person or thing doing something? No, it doesn't. Does it have a predicate? Maybe *raining* is a predicate. We can't be sure. It is not a complete sentence.

Be sure all your sentences have a subject and a predicate.

Writing Paragraphs

A paragraph is a group of sentences about the same topic. The first sentence tells the topic. The rest of the sentences tell more about the topic. The first sentence in a paragraph is indented. That means it starts a little to the right.

Read this paragraph.

I like July best. It is warm in July. My family goes to the lake. We watch fireworks. <u>My best friend likes December</u>. We eat ice cream and drink lemonade. July is my favorite month.

The topic is the main idea of the paragraph. It is in the first sentence. The first sentence is indented. The rest of the sentences tell more about the topic.

Read the underlined sentence. It doesn't tell about the topic. Let's take out that sentence.

I like July best. It is warm in July. My family goes to the lake. We watch fireworks. We eat ice cream and drink lemonade. July is my favorite month.

Now we have a good paragraph.

Action Words

Read these two sentences. Which one is more interesting?

> Jake <u>fell</u> to the ground.
>
> Jake <u>tumbled</u> to the ground.

The second sentence is more interesting. The word *tumbled* means the same thing as the word *fell,* but it tells more. The word *tumbled* gives a picture. Try using a special book to find good action words. The special book is called a *thesaurus.* See page HB 18 for information about using a thesaurus.

Describing Words

Read these two sentences. Which one has more details?

> Emily carried a balloon.
>
> Emily carried a <u>shiny</u>, <u>new</u>, <u>red</u> balloon.

The first sentence doesn't have any details. The second sentence has a lot of details. It tells that the balloon was shiny, new, and red. Describing words tell how something looks, sounds, smells, feels, or tastes. Describing words will make your writing more interesting.

Revising
Add and Take Out

Using a Dictionary

A dictionary is a book of words. It has the spellings and meanings of words. A dictionary is a good tool for writers. It can help you spell words. It can also help you learn new words.

Look inside a dictionary. You will see that the words are in columns. The words go from the top of the page to the bottom. Then the columns go from the left side of the page to the right side. Words in a dictionary are in ABC order. Be sure you understand what words mean and use the right meanings of words when you write.

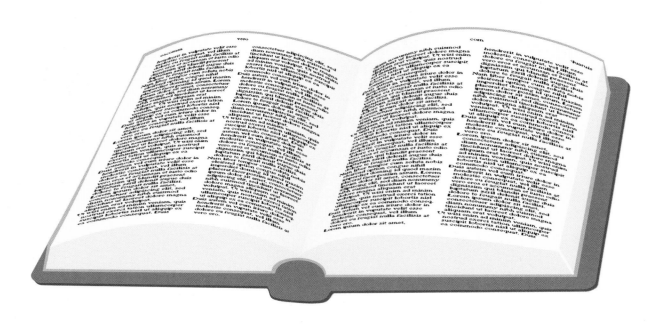

Using a Thesaurus

A thesaurus is a special kind of book. It has all kinds of words. A thesaurus has words that mean the same thing. It also has words that mean the opposite. Words in a thesaurus are in ABC order. A thesaurus can help make your writing more interesting. Read this paragraph.

My sister Morgan likes all kinds of fruit. She will eat peaches and pears. She will eat apples, bananas, and grapes. She will also eat plums and oranges. I can't think of any fruit Morgan won't eat.

Does this paragraph seem kind of boring? That's because we used the word *eat* too many times. A thesaurus has many words that mean the same thing as *eat*. You might find the words *munch, gobble, chomp,* and *nibble* in a thesaurus. Let's use some of those words in place of *eat* in our paragraph. Read the new paragraph on the next page.

My sister Morgan likes all kinds of fruit. She will **munch** peaches and pears. She will **gobble** apples, bananas, and grapes. She will also **chomp** plums and oranges. I can't think of any fruit Morgan won't **nibble**.

Now our paragraph is colorful and rich. Try using a thesaurus when you get stuck with the same word. Use it to learn new words, too.

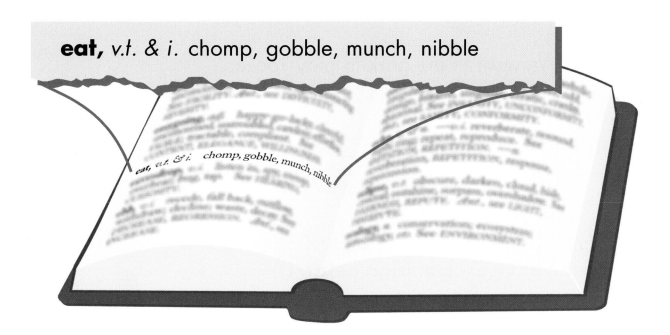

eat, *v.t. & i.* chomp, gobble, munch, nibble

Sentences

Capitalization

Every sentence begins with a **capital letter**.

The sun is out today.

End Marks

Every sentence ends with a **punctuation mark**.
Sentences that tell end with a period. **(.)**

We went to the park to play soccer**.**

Sentences that ask a question end with a
question mark. **(?)**

Was it hot at the park**?**

Sentences that show strong feelings
end with an **exclamation point**. **(!)**

No, it was a great day**!**

Subjects and Predicates

A sentence is a group of words that tells a complete thought. A sentence has a **subject** and a **predicate**.

The subject is the "doer" in the sentence. It is the person or the thing that does something.

> **Our soccer team** won the game.

The predicate tells what the subject is doing.

> Our soccer team **won the game**.

Quotation Marks

Quotation marks separate someone's words from the rest of the sentence. They are used to show conversation in stories.

> Jordan said, "I have a baby sister."

Contractions

Contractions are a short way of writing or saying two words. When we put two words together in writing to make a contraction, we use an **apostrophe (')** to replace the dropped letters.

do	+	not	=	don't		she	+	is	=	she's
can	+	not	=	can't		he	+	has	=	he's
will	+	not	=	won't		they	+	will	=	they'll

Parts of Speech

Nouns

Nouns are words that name people, places, and things.

A **singular noun** names one person, place, or thing.

boy	house	bus
girl	town	car
box	bench	dress

A **plural noun** names more than one person, place, or thing. We usually add *-s* to a noun to make it plural. If a noun ends in *s, ch, sh,* or *x,* we add *-es* to make it plural.

boys	houses	buses
girls	towns	cars
boxes	benches	dresses

Pronouns

Pronouns take the place of nouns.

I	he	she
me	it	you
we	they	us

Verbs

Verbs are words that show action.

    play   talk   read

Some verbs do not show action.

    is   was   are

Verbs can show the present, the past, or the future.

Present	Past	Future
talk	talked	will talk
play	played	will play

Adjectives

Adjectives describe nouns and pronouns. They tell how something looks, feels, sounds, tastes, and smells.

blue	quiet	soft
sweet	tall	loud

Adverbs

Adverbs usually describe verbs. They tell how, when, where, or how much. Many adverbs end with -*ly*.

quickly	slowly	nicely
carefully	happily	cheerfully